To Pam...
Enjoy!!!
Hagmeyer 1/29/1

Stumbling Over A Quarter To Pick Up A Penny

Understanding Your Life's Six Spiritual Periods

"Blessed is the man who does not walk in the counsel of the wicked or stand in the way of sinners or sit in the seat of mockers. But his delight is in the law of the LORD, and on His law he meditates day and night. He is like a tree planted by streams of water, which yields its fruit in season and whose leaf does not wither. Whatever he does prospers." (Psalms 1:1-3)

Hayward C. Townsend Sr.

Featuring your own

Determining Your Life's Spiritual Period Worksheet

*Stumbling Over A Quarter To Pick Up A Penny:Understanding
Your Life's Six Spiritual Periods*
© *2009 Hayward C. Townsend Sr.. All rights reserved.*

AuthorHouse™
1663 Liberty Drive
Bloomington, IN 47403
www.authorhouse.com
Phone: 1-800-839-8640

No part of this book may be reproduced, stored in a retrieval system, or transmitted by any means without the written permission of the author.

First published by AuthorHouse 8/14/2009

ISBN: 978-1-4490-0855-0 (e)
ISBN: 978-1-4490-0853-6 (sc)
ISBN: 978-1-4490-0854-3 (hc)

Scripture quotations marked "KJV" are taken from the Holy Bible, King James Version, Cambridge, 1769.

Printed in the United States of America
Bloomington, Indiana

This book is printed on acid-free paper.

Dedication

I dedicate this book with great respect and love to:

*My parents, Joe L. Townsend Sr.
and Bertha M. Townsend for preparing me well for life's journey.*

*My beautiful wife, Barbara,
for always being there to encourage me in everything that I do.*

*My daughter and son, Dorian and Chip,
for adding joy and purpose to my life.*

I also dedicate this book with special thanks and gratitude to:

*My sister Overseer Marion Douglas,
because she is always "in the middle" with me.*

*My spiritual cover, Dr. Bill Adkins Jr.,
for generously providing me the opportunities
to practice what I preach.*

Finally, I dedicate this book with Honor to:

My GOD, through whom all blessings flow.

In the Bible in Exodus 10:2, the Lord told Moses that He gave the Children of Israel the wonderful stories about how He hardened Pharaoh's heart and then delivered them from Pharaoh's wrath so that they could tell those stories to their children to make them know and love Him and identify His works. Likewise, the stories in this book are about the experiences that God gave me when I had hardened my heart and turned my back on Him. I'm sure that He wants me to use them to pass the wisdom contained in them on to you, my children, my grandchildren and future generations so that we all can love Him and identify His work in our lives. Just as the Children of Israel's stories are not just stories about them, my stories are not just about me; they are about God and the lessons that He wants to use them to teach.

The stories in this book are from years ago and are built around a recent awareness that God gave me of how to unlock the understanding of life's **Six Spiritual Periods: Probation, Preparation, Conquest, Power, Decline and Servitude.** It is an understanding that I use everyday to capture and maintain the stability of God's **Power** in my life and the lives of those around me. In the chapters of this book, I'll explain to you what life's **Six Spiritual Periods** are and give you simple tools to use to identify the period that you are in so that you too can unlock a world of extraordinary achievement. I'll show you how to use that understanding to properly leverage your situations and examine with you some of the consequences that will occur in your life when you take a wrong action because you don't know or incorrectly identify the period that you are in. Finally, and most importantly, we'll look and see what scripture and other bits of wisdom are tied to each period that you can internalize and later act on to stay in God's **Power ... that place in your life where you experience victory after victory regardless of your circumstances.**

As you read this book, you will see that by the time I was 25 years old I had made many more BIG mistakes than most individuals have made by the time that they are twice that age. So laugh at the stories as I now do ... and your laughter will lighten your heart and help to bring you an understanding of life's **Six Spiritual Periods**.

The events that reward us in our life don't occur all at once but rather they come together like a 500-piece puzzle that finally shows itself when we are over halfway finished and well past the point where we would tear it apart and put it back in the box. So remember the information that explains the various periods ... apply it in your life and it will help you to avoid some of life's pitfalls and to rise out of them when you find yourself struggling inside of them. When you've finished reading ... identify your current **Spiritual Period,** apply the appropriate scriptural-based actions that are discussed at the end of each chapter and then enjoy the personal happiness fostered by your new understanding of how God's **Power** works.

As you read the stories, you'll see that more often than not my actions were not in synch with what I should have been doing based on what the word of God requires for the **Spiritual Period** that I was in. You'll see that at best, my actions were futile. They were like having the positive and negative ends of two magnets too far apart to attract each other. They often became too separated from God's Will and I couldn't determine the actions that I needed to take to connect to His **Power.**

During most of these stories, I stayed out of God's **Power** until I acknowledged and confessed my shortcomings, accepted God's **Probation** and yielded to His authority. Whenever I did not accept God's authority there was no **Conquest** in my life and I slid into **Decline** and lived in **Servitude.** Most of the time, although I looked and felt prosperous, I wasn't because I had turned my back on God's blessings and favor and was just *Stumbling Over A Quarter To Pick Up A Penny.*

While in a period of **Power** God revealed to me how to understand and use the knowledge of life's **Six Spiritual Periods: Probation, Preparation, Conquest, Power, Decline, and Servitude** to stay in His **Power** or quickly return to it when I unknowingly let my life slip into **Decline** or fall into **Servitude.**

He'll show you too. Just finish reading the stories and complete the *Determining Your Life's Spiritual Period Worksheet* at the end of the book ... **it's just that simple**. But let's first get started by looking to see why, if God's blessing is a quarter, I was so willing to stumble over it and pick up the penny.

Hayward C. Townsend Sr.
Arlington, Tennessee

Contents

Introduction: Homeless 1

1. **Decline:** May I Help You? 9

2. **Servitude:** Lying at First Light 19

3. **Probation:** The Psychic Plowboys Experience 31

4. **Preparation:** Baby Eagles and Piano Lessons 39

5. **Conquest:** Can You Hold Your Breath? 47

6. **Power:** Riding to the Games 55

7. **Conclusion:** How Do You Do It? 71

8. **Steps to Using the Understanding of the Six Spiritual Periods** 75

Determining Your Life's Spiritual Period Worksheet 87

Pictures 91

Endnotes 101

Acknowledgements 103

Introduction

Homeless

You learn a lot when you are homeless ... like how to use a good cedar tree and a little waxed cardboard to protect yourself from the bitter cold and the pouring rain ... you learn which Christian mission soup kitchens serve the best free meals with the least hassle. You also learn how to make it to the temporary employment office by 4:30 in the morning so that you can be in the front of the line to get one of the "best" day laborer jobs that they have listed. The "best" day labor job in Memphis, at that time in 1977, meant that you wouldn't have to dig raw sewage by hand with a shovel out of a pit like I had to do when I got to the temporary employment office after 4:30 and was assigned to work at the Dehyco Company located 6 blocks south of downtown just southwest of the corner of Florida Street and McLemore Avenue. The "best" day labor job meant that since I could read, if I got there by 4:30, I could get a job that day working in a warehouse picking or packing orders for the minimum wage of what was then $2.30 an hour. You see ... in my case, I wasn't the 4:30 early bird that got up early to catch the worm ... I was the early bird that got up early to get picked for a warehouse job that would let me hold on to a little bit of my almost totally depleted pride.

When you're homeless ... your list of needs get real short. You learn how to create and implement schemes to get yourself the situation-adjusted list of life essentials that you feel that you need. You devise schemes like the one where I would go to the Memphis State University Student Center (currently the University of Memphis) in East Memphis, and tell the clerk at the desk, "I just lost fifty-cents in the snack machine." Although I wasn't a student, since I knew how to look the part of a student, she would give me the money and never question me. That was one of my quick and clean schemes that would always net me enough money to buy a McDonald's hamburger or almost a third of the money I needed to purchase my always-present half pint of E & J Brandy.

After picking up the snack machine money, some days while I was still on the university campus, I would use another scheme where I would go to the Student Recreation and Fitness Center that was located south of the main campus and across the Southern Avenue railroad tracks. There I would play handball, use the sauna and take a shower. You see ... while the cedar trees did protect me from the elements, there were no showers under them and I needed to have reasonable good hygiene and look like a student for most of my schemes to work. By the way ... those two schemes were universal and they worked just as effectively at the University of Southern California when I was out there in 1978 as they did when I used them in Memphis at Memphis State.

For thousands of years, small groups of people have chosen to be homeless nomads such as the Romani people (Gypsies) of Eastern Europe, the Middle Eastern Bedouins and members of other subcultures of the world. I realize now that this was a time in my life where I had chosen to be a nomad and to be homeless by turning my back on the blessings and favor of God. It was a time when I was ... **Stumbling Over A Quarter To Pick up A Penny**. It was readily apparent to myself and others while I slept under trees, schemed, lied, stole, rolled drunks and did all of my shysting that I was "physically homeless". What I didn't realize until much later was that I had become "spiritually homeless" long before I became "physically homeless". I had squandered most of the power that God had provided for me through caring parents, grandparents, close family members, teachers, friends and others by getting into relationships that altered my personality and turned my focus away from God.

Some of you who are reading this book are *homeless* today. Even though you are sitting in your secure house, just finished eating a great meal and are kicking your feet up to do a little reading, watch a show from your favorite television series or maybe balance your checkbook. Do you want to know if you are "spiritually homeless" or on your way there? If you do, ask yourself this question: **Do I sometimes have the feeling that although my life seems to be going perfectly well that there is something that is**

still just not right? What I'm asking you is do you often feel incomplete although you have acquired material wealth and even accomplished much, much more than what you expected that you would after having experienced disappointing times earlier in your life. Do you feel that you should be doing more? And you just can't put your finger on what is causing you to feel the way that you do ... but all you know is that that nagging incompleteness won't leave you no matter how successful you are and no matter how God has blessed you and your family.

When I began to write this book a few years ago, that's the exact state of mind that I was in. God had delivered me again and again from my "physical homeless" experiences but I wasn't satisfied and I didn't feel complete. I was respected in my church, on my job, in the community and by individuals around the world in the places I had traveled to. How could I be harboring that feeling of incompleteness? I see now that my problem was that I hadn't realized and accepted the fact that God, through Jesus, had delivered me from being "spiritually homeless" and even though I was constantly surrounded with the evidence that He had done so I didn't realize that He had.

As I said earlier, wherever I went I was respected. Mr. Veltman, then a 70-year old Dutch agnostic community leader, told me that he respected my insight on world events and religion when we had discussed them at his home in Tilburg, The Netherlands in the fall of 1994. During a religious and humanitarian mission to Ghana in the fall of 2003, I had enjoyed discussing with several prominent Ghanaians possible solutions to the agricultural, health and other socio-economics issues that have persisted in their country since independence from the United Kingdom was won there in 1957. Many people spoke highly of me but the feeling of incompleteness would not leave me. In fact, my life was going so well that people were giving me credit for accomplishing things that I didn't do ... but my feeling of incompleteness would not go away.

Wow! Here I was in a place in life where twenty years ago I had tried every manipulative technique that I could imagine, create or uncover and I still could only get vestiges of these types of accomplishments to happen in my life. What was the difference between my period of success now, wrapped in emptiness as it was, and my failures twenty years ago? It was that now, even though I didn't realize it, I was in God's **Power** ... back then I was not. Now, whatever

Stumbling Over A Quarter To Pick Up A Penny

I attempted was successful. Back then, practically everything I tried failed. I hadn't learned that sometimes you need to slow down to speed up. Even seeing men stabbed over less than ten dollars and later witnessing the cold-blooded murder of a good man over a pawned gun while pulling off a couple of my schemes had not persuaded me to slow down and take account of those experiences and learn from the lessons that they contained.

Except for my homeless years, I have always excelled. Made lots of money. Lived in the best places. Drove the best cars. At nineteen, I had a condo in the Hamlets, a high-end complex in the then newly developed community which at that time was just outside of the Memphis southeast city limits. At 23 years old, I owned a triple gray Corvette Stingray car, had finished requirements to go to medical school and was traveling around the world playing music.

I started my first non-profit organization, the Young People's Association of America (YPA), at the age of twenty-four. For the YPA's first major project, I wrote a proposal to obtain grant-based funding for a million and a half dollar drug and alcohol rehabilitation center for Memphis through the Comprehensive Employment and Training Act (CETA) program. While the proposal made it through the preliminary screening on the strength of it concept, I had no idea that the powers-to-be were not going to fund any proposal from a non-politically connected twenty-four year old. Boy was I naïve ... but if I hadn't been so naïve I would have missed the opportunity to learn skills that I have used continuously since then. Oh by the way ... they took the grant money and funded a program that cleaned grass, debris and junk from vacant inner city lots.

But for now let's get back to the point. Back then, during my *homeless* period, like a lot of people today, when it came to recognizing God's sovereignty working in my life I didn't realize that I needed to respond to it based on an understanding of the **Six Spiritual Periods** of life. I rationalized my lifestyle's hedonistic thoughts and behavior; that got in the way of my understanding and I became "spiritually homeless" ... disconnected from God's **Power**. Today, now that I've grasped an understanding of the **Six Spiritual Periods** I know how to use that knowledge to avoid any feeling of incompleteness and stay connected to God's **Power**. When I have a drop in power I get connected again ... and I do it without it having to take me months of confusion or years of pain like it did in the past. I'll show you how to grasp that understanding too.

Let's get started.

The Six Spiritual Periods

On a piece of paper write down the ***Six Spiritual Periods: Probation, Preparation, Conquest, Power, Decline, and Servitude.*** Memorize them.

Next ... here are a few facts that you need to be aware of about the **Six Spirituals Periods**.

- There is no set order that you will experience the **Six Spiritual Periods**. For example, you may be in **Preparation** in your youth and also in your middle age.

- You experience a particular period based on your awareness and understanding of what is currently happening in your life. For example, if you are in **Power** and don't realize it your experiences won't be as rewarding for you as they could be.

- You move from one period to another or remain in the current period that you are in based on the actions that you take. If you take the correct action you can move into the positive periods of **Preparation**, **Conquest** or stay in **Power**. In these three periods God allows mostly positive tests into your life to get you to accomplish His Will.

- When you are in **Preparation**, **Conquest** or **Power** and you take the incorrect action you won't be able to avoid one or all of the periods of **Decline**, **Servitude**, and **Probation**. They are the periods where God allows mostly not so positive tests and trials to occur for you in order to get you back on track to accomplish His Will.

- The majority of the time in your life when you are ***Stumbling Over A Quarter To Pick Up A Penny*** you are: 1) Out of synch with God's sovereign plan for you; 2) Acting or reacting improperly according to the **Spiritual Period** that you are in at that time and; 3)

Have turned your back on God's blessings and favor. You may not be completely outside of His Will ... just responding and reacting improperly to it. I'll discuss how all of this works in greater detail later.

What **Spiritual Period** are you in? Read the following list and use the information in it to determine the period that you are in based on what's happening in your life.

Period	What is God Doing To Or For You
Probation	God is challenging you to get rid of your self-defeating habits
Preparation	God is preparing you to meet life's conquests
Conquest	God is allowing you to expand and grow into **Power**
Power	God is allowing you to achieve victory after victory
Decline	God is allowing your victories to end because you have stopped taking the actions necessary to keep you in His **Power**
Servitude	God is allowing difficulties and decay to enter into your life because you are letting Satan set your agenda

Probation, Preparation, Conquest and **Power** are the periods where God wants something from you or of you. You may be in His Will but not totally aligned to it. Ask yourself these questions: What is it that God wants of me? What should I be doing if I am in **Probation** ... or **Preparation** ... or **Conquest?** If I'm not in God's **Power** how do I get there and remain there? If I'm in God's Power why do I want to remain there?

Decline and **Servitude** are the periods that you find yourself in when you are knowingly or unknowingly *not* doing or attempting to do what God wants you to do. Ask yourself this question: Am I outside of God's Will for me? Then find out if you are by asking yourself the following questions: Are the majority of my actions contrary to the nature, character and Will of God? You're asking yourself ... am I sinning? Are my actions about me or about God? You're asking yourself ... am I selfish? If you answered either one of the last four questions 'yes' then you are outside of God's Will and you are in **Decline** or **Servitude**. What should you do now that you've determined that you are in **Decline** or **Servitude**? How do you get to God's **Power** from there?

There are numerous other questions about the **Six Spiritual Periods** that need asking and answering and I'll cover them in the chapters to come. But for right now ... just imagine that you are like I was as a young man and you can't recognize the **Spiritual Period** that you are in because you are unaware that they exist. You are unknowingly making all of the wrong choices and missing opportunities to react properly to situations when God wants to bless you. Imagine that you are me in 1976, ***Stumbling Over A Quarter To Pick Up A Penny.***

Let's begin our understanding of life's **Six Spiritual Periods** with a story about the **Decline** period. While **Decline** is not necessarily the beginning period of the **Six Spiritual Periods** it's where we'll start because you're usually well into it before you realize that you are.

Chapter One

Decline: May I Help You?

If you try hard enough you can pin-point an exact moment when you realize that you were turning away from God ... not completely turned away but turning away from Him. It's that time in your life when what you are doing has stopped working for you. It's the point when you are no longer in God's **Power** but beginning to enter a **Decline** period in your life.

For me, it was about 9:30 one overcast fall morning in 1976. I remember pulling my gray Corvette way too fast into the parking lot of what was then The Treasury Store. The Treasury Store was a subsidiary of the JCPenny Company and was located on the southwest corner of Elvis Presley Blvd and Holmes Road in the Southwest Memphis community called Whitehaven. It had a full-service grocery store under the same roof as a major retail department store. There was a full-service gas station island out front. It was one of those stores that helped to pioneer the concept that Wal-Mart uses so profitably today.

The gas pump attendant was a man in his late forties with red hair and a red beard that was peppered with gray. He was a skinny man about six feet tall and looked to weigh about 140 pounds. He had on a dingy, short-sleeved shirt that looked beige but you could see that at some time earlier it had been white. On the right side of the shirt, opposite the store logo and inside of an embroidered red oval, was the name Earl. Earl had on navy blue pants that had black grease around the top of the side pockets and on the knees. The pants hung down over his beat-up brown work boots. He was chewing a big wad of tobacco and a small stream of juice was running out of one of the corners of his mouth. I could tell that he wasn't comfortable with the idea of providing full service for me on my expensive sports car. He was supposed to check my oil level, the air in my tires and clean my windshield while he pumped my gas but

Stumbling Over A Quarter To Pick Up A Penny

I could tell that if anything got cleaned or checked in the next 10 minutes it would be me doing the cleaning and the checking.

Anyway, once Earl composed himself he walked up to my car, looked at me and said, "May I help you?" Now, since my JCPenny credit card was maxed out and would have been declined I couldn't say, "fill her up" so I said, "Yeah, you can help me ... can you pump me one dollar worth of regular?" and handed him a crisp one dollar bill through my window. He froze still and didn't make a move to pump my gas. From the sudden gleam in his earlier dull eyes, a new smirk on his mouth and the twitch of his left jaw, I could tell that I had just given him the opening that he needed to get into my business ... and he proceeded to try to take a little wind out of my sail. "I wouldn't have a car like that", he said, "if I couldn't afford gas for it".

Now I can't tell you what I said to him at that time for two reasons. One was because what I said was purely reactionary and I don't remember exactly what I said. The other is because I can no longer repeat the part that I do remember, but I'm sure he heard me because after he told me "where to go", he crumpled up the dollar bill and threw it back at me through my t-top. He didn't know that I was "on my way there" anyway and that I didn't need his directions. He just knew where to hit me though and the blow that he delivered to my pride was devastating because it was true.

The gas station attendant had picked up on the fact that my briefly-enjoyed **Power** period of the past few years was over and that my life was in **Decline** and headed towards **Servitude**. Everyone that I came into contact during that time knew that except me. I was in denial and I didn't want to give up any ground. But the fact is that **Decline** usually follows **Power** and since I had eliminated the behavior that kept me in God's **Power**, I was no longer there and hadn't been there for quite some time. I had stopped practicing the habits that helped me stay in **Power**; I had stopped going to worship service, attending my college classes regularly, and I no longer had gainful employment. I was focusing on my present position in life and not focusing on the future that God had prepared me for.

I had allowed other peoples' opinions and mores to dictate my life and was too conflicted to tell myself "Hayward ... you are not in **Power** when you have an expensive car and can't afford gas for it. You are not in **Power** when you are hiding your car to keep it from being repossessed. You are not in **Power** when you feel the need to lie to yourself and others about anything and everything. You are not in **Power** when what you are accomplishing causes you to sin against God or cause others to sin against Him ... you are in **Decline**."

My above story leads to the following important fact about being in a **Decline** period in your life:

You enter into a Decline period in your life when you stop doing the things that keep you in God's Power.

How Are Your Habits?

Many people go into **Decline** periods in their life unaware, as I had done during this stage in my life. You give up your "good practices", the group of essential habits that keep you in God's **Power**. Practices like: taking time for your morning prayer, having private time with God, and showing up to the midweek worship service that re-charges your faith and keeps you spiritually connected. You stop volunteering to help others. You become callous and you begin to ignore or justify the hurt that your actions and the actions of others cause God's people.

When you are in **Decline** you find ways to start removing the positive influences that exist in your life ... the one's that God put there to help you to succeed. You get too smart to be involved in any type of organized learning and you stop participating in any form of organized meetings. You ignore an import rule for personal and spiritual growth that says, "If you are always the wisest person in all of the meetings that you attend then you need to attend some different meetings". You abhor discipline of any kind and unknowingly you have created the perfect environment to one day find yourself physically and spiritually homeless.

Every time that you quit doing the behavior that keeps you in **Power** you go into a **Decline** period in your life. In the Bible, the Children of Israel were notorious for exhibiting this type of behavior. They worshipped God and then they stopped worshipping Him and worshipped Baal the Semitic god of the Canaanites and Phoenicians. Then they worshipped God and then they worshipped Asherah the goddess, the Queen of heaven, whose worship Jeremiah so vehemently opposed. They didn't stop there; they worshipped other pagan gods too. It was during the quitting of their worship to God that they entered into **Decline**. The problem was that they had grown to know that they needed to worship something and every time they stopped worshipping God they filled the void by worshipping the gods of their pagan neighbors. We do that too.

You remain in a Decline period because you isolate yourself from "good people" ... and soon the way that you conduct yourself is contrary to what is written in Scripture.

Two years prior to the beginning of my **Decline** period that I wrote about above, I began to gradually isolate myself from my family and before long I was completely isolated from them. I see now that one of my biggest mistakes during this period was not communicating with them. By not doing so, I had no one to tell me that I was making immature mistakes. I probably wouldn't have listened ... but that's not the point. The point is that I needed to hear from someone that my behavior wasn't right and I didn't. I didn't hear what I needed to hear because the people that I had surrounded myself with didn't consider the hedonism and depravity that we were involved in to be contrary to what God required of us in His Word.

I've read that Dale Carnegie, as successful as he was, didn't complete college, but he had two life-long habits that compensated for that: He never isolated himself to one way of thinking and he was not willing to be stopped by his failures ... he was always willing to learn from them. I just couldn't see that far. At that time I did neither.

Today, we have to be aware and not become isolated and controlled by various authors, ministers, media and others who build our world view and influence our thoughts and belief away from God's truth. By isolating myself I invited **Decline**. Very seldom, if ever, can you isolate yourself and get the information that you need. The Bible says in Hebrew 10:25, "Let us not give up meeting together, as some are in the habit of doing, but let us encourage one another." I should have known this scripture and understood its importance.

Also when you isolate yourself you are more prone to start listening to gossips and other negative people. There is an explicit warning about listening and associating with them in Proverbs 16:28, "A perverse man stirs up dissension, and a gossip separates close friends."

Decline always leads to Servitude.

Do You Really Fear God?

When you are in **Decline** you forget your life's past accomplishments, ignore today's celebrations and run exhaustively toward an unstable future. In fact, you are running so fast that you find yourself ***Stumbling Over A Quarter To Pick Up A Penny***. What will happen? What will the end result be? It will be that you will find that you are no longer in **Decline** but that you have made your way to **Servitude** and will have to deal with the harsh consequences of the selfish and sinful changes that you have allowed to occur in your behavior, habits and practices.

You never go directly from the **Power** period or any other period to a **Servitude** period. You always go through **Decline** to get there. The Children of Israel, even though they were God's Chosen People and spent a lot of time in **Servitude** periods, they never went directly from **Power** to **Servitude**. Even during the 350 years when they were led by Judges they were in **Servitude** only approximately 100 years. During the other 250 years they vacillated between the other five **Spiritual Periods** based on how they responded to the directions provided to them from God through their leaders. But one common thread is that when they found themselves in **Decline** periods they could never stop the slide into **Servitude** once they got on that slippery slope.

What behavior caused them to go into **Decline**? They did several things. One was that they consciously stopped fearing God and then always compounded the problem by worshipping idols and other gods. Believe it or not ... our actions prove that you and I sometimes subconsciously stop fearing God and in some cases we never feared Him at all. How do we stop fearing God? We do it knowingly or unknowingly by beginning to worship the idols (people, homes, jewelry, jobs and other stuff) of our life rather than God and that behavior puts us on a slippery slope just like the one that led the ancient Israelites and me ... into **Decline**.

When I was in this **Decline** period, I don't believe that I consciously stopped fearing God I just got out of touch with Him because he was out of my sight. I believe that I could have avoided the slippery slope that led me into **Servitude** if I had had the following scriptures internalized. One scripture reads, "The fear of the Lord is the beginning of knowledge, but fools *(ones who are morally deficient)* despise wisdom and discipline." Proverbs 1:7 (emphasis added). The other one is Proverbs 15:16 which reads, "Better a little with the fear of the LORD than great wealth with turmoil."

When you are in Decline check your direction and see if you can still see God in everything or whether you are focused on some other god.

Remember that we've already discussed that **Servitude** periods are preceded by periods of **Decline** so how do you recognize that you are entering into a **Decline** period? How does it happen? Why can't you just stop it when it starts? What are the little changes in the patterns of your life that you need to look for?

Let's look at some of them.

You need to begin by looking for a long ago suppressed insecure, jealous, envious or selfish spirit to resurface. You need to determine if you have become depraved and are now letting your personal pursuit of sexual and material gratifications occupy your time and purposes. Has your list of *wants* grown too large and you have subconsciously begun to let it dictate how you spend your time and your wealth? Do ulterior motives dictate your actions? For example, if you are in **Decline** even when you attend church you have ulterior motives and those motives, not the worship of God, dictate what you do. You'll let your hedonistic thoughts and actions control you because you have yielded to the philosophy that pleasure is your most important pursuit. You sing in the choir because you know how to find your pleasures there ... or you might go to the gym not really to exercise but because you can sneak a perverted peak at someone of the opposite sex or maybe because you are on the prowl to find your next sexual partner.

Even your choice of careers can be dictated by insincere motives when you are in a period of **Decline**. Some masseuses only choose that profession so that they can have the sexual gratification of putting their hands on individuals without being encumbered by societal rules. Some pedophiles teach elementary school to be near a seemingly in-exhaustive supply of children approaching puberty. Some ministers only preach so that they can use the power of the pulpit to fulfill their selfish desires. In **Decline**, just like them, you become jaded, cynical, callous and worn out.

If you are not careful, before too long the subconscious pursuit of these life altering goals are setting your agenda without you even being aware of the change of your life's course. In other words, you have allowed Satan to set your agenda and when you do your life will lose its focus. You will not see God because you have turned your back on Him and are ***Stumbling Over A Quarter To Pick Up A Penny.*** Your power is gone and you are deep in **Decline**.

The best way to get out of a Decline period is to never get into one in the first place and you accomplish that by taking the actions that will keep you in God's Power.

Unfortunately, since never getting into a period of **Decline** is virtually impossible for all of us to do the next best solution is to know what actions we need to focus on to get out of one when we find ourselves there.

Your first action in **Decline** is for you to recognize that you are no longer in God's **Power** and then focus on taking the actions that will get you into a **Preparation** period. You need to start developing new habits and acquiring new wisdom while at the same time ridding yourself of the depravity that is preventing you from holding on to that which is good. You must do what the Bible says in Hebrews 12:1-2, "Therefore, since we have so great a cloud of witnesses surrounding us, let us also lay aside every encumbrance and the sin which so easily entangles us, and let us run with endurance the race that is set before us, fixing our eyes on Jesus, the author and perfecter of faith …".

You need to also closely analyze your motives for going the places that you go and for the actions you take once you get there. Ask yourself, "Am I doing this for God or am I doing this to satisfy one of my ulterior motives?" Ask yourself, "Am I moving away from a depraved state or moving towards one?" Ask yourself, "Am I becoming less jaded, cynical and callous and fixing my eyes on Jesus the author and perfecter of my faith?"

To get out of a Decline period you need to refocus your energy towards God and wait for Him to move you into a period of Preparation.

Don't Keep The Spoils

To determine how to refocus let's investigate what the Children of Israel did when God moved them into **Preparation** from **Decline.** First, they stopped worshipping idol gods and tore down the altars they had set up to honor them. Next, they started again to follow God's law to the detail. They also didn't keep any of the previous habits or *spoils* from their previous existence unless they knew that God approved of it. In the Bible in 1 Samuels Chapter 15, there is the story about Saul, the first king of Israel, who in his arrogance and disobedience, kept *spoils* from the nations that God had allowed him to conquer. In one instance, although God had given him specific instructions to destroy everything associated with the city of Amalek he kept some of the *spoils* of his victory. He also, in further disobedience, allowed Agag the king of the Amalekites to live. These and later egregious actions on Saul's part led to his decline and the decline of those he ruled over. The nation of Israel soon found themselves defeated by the Philistines and in **Servitude** to them. They stayed in that position of **Servitude** until Saul's death and King David's subsequent rule. Are you keeping *spoils* acquired during a **Decline** period that you still need to discard?

In this story you see that you must not keep unquieted *spoils* as Saul did because you not only place yourself in **Servitude** but those who look to you for strength as well. You must do as David did after Saul's death when he ruled first in Hebron and later in Jerusalem. In Hebron, he established a place for the Nation of Israel to wait for God to move them into **Preparation** and later in Jerusalem he built a stronghold where they could worship God and live as he knew they should. There in Jerusalem they prepared for God to move them into **Conquest** and when He did they conquered all of their enemies and received the blessings that had been promised to them from the time of their father Abraham.

When the events of the above story played out in my life I was in deep **Decline**. I was failing in strength and wounded in spirit and just as David wrote in Psalms 31:1 ... I needed a refuge. Sometimes mental or physical illnesses can bring on a **Decline** period but that wasn't the case for me. I had chosen to do what Saul did rather than what David did and God had chosen to move me from **Decline** into **Servitude**.

Next let's talk about **Servitude** ... that place where you don't want to be but more often than not you find yourself in at some point in your life.

Chapter Two

Servitude: Lying at First Light

No one expected John Butler to shoot and kill Alvi Smith at the small joint that Alvi owned on Highway 64 in Oakland, Tennessee approximately 30 miles east of Memphis. Everyone thought that John was all bark and no bite. But on that late summer Saturday morning in 1979 John Butler showed everyone that what they thought about him was very, very wrong.

I was there when Alvi died and the reason why I was there shows how, with help, I had progressed to bigger schemes than driving around in a soon-to-be-repossessed Corvette, living exclusively off of credit cards and collecting funds for non-existent charities. On that morning we, Cornell Taylor, his cousin Sam Taylor and I, were there trying to work out a way to get the musical sound equipment we needed to perform an outdoors concert for the Holly Springs Motorcycle Club. It was supposed to take place on the club's 20-acre campground in Byhalia, Mississippi about 20 miles south of Oakland. The fee that we had charged them was $600 dollars and we had collected a $300 deposit several months ago.

This story should have been uneventful and no one should have died. It should have gone something like this ... we sign the contract, and play the concert, collect the remainder of our fee and go home like normal bands do. But when you are in **Servitude** nothing happens quite as simple as it should. We had told one of our usual lies, a big lie, and when we signed the contract we had sold ourselves as a full seven-piece band by using another band's literature and picture. In fact, when we signed the contract there were just the three of us ... Cornell on electric guitar, Sam our one-handed conga player who whistled and me who played acoustic guitar. We had a total of about 19 years musical experience ... but there was one problem and that problem was that I had 18 of those years of experience and my experience was on the drums not on the acoustic guitar which I planned on playing for the concert.

Stumbling Over A Quarter To Pick Up A Penny

Now, this wouldn't be our first concert. We had done impromptu concerts for our family and friends until they stopped letting us visit them when we had our instruments with us. Some family members let us visit when we brought our instruments if we promised to not sing or whistle. Other family members would just turn out the lights and not answer the door when we showed up. Before that morning, we had also played one other aborted concert in North Memphis at a club on the corner of Firestone and Thomas a few blocks north of downtown in the heart of the ghetto. It was on a Friday evening. Things didn't go well at all and what happened that evening is another story.

Anyway, here we are that overcast morning, stuck in our lie and trying to recover from it. I was praying for rain so that the concert would be canceled, but I wasn't really expecting it to rain. To make matters worse, we had already spent the $300 retainer fee so we couldn't back out of the concert. So we were going to have to do the concert and make the best of it or try to avoid about 200 bikers as long as we lived in Memphis.

Alvi had an 8-channel Peavy PA system, speakers, monitors, microphones and other equipment that we were going to try to rent and use to bluff our way through the concert. What we planned to do was to show up, set up the equipment and screech the microphones with feedback for a few minutes. We were then going to blow some fuses on the system and then say that the available power wouldn't support the equipment. We felt that we could pull it off because we had had a lot of success with lying and besides no one was as smart as we were. We were in **Servitude** and when you are in **Servitude** you think that no one ... I mean no one ... is as smart as you.

We got to Alvi's Place at around 9 o'clock that morning and pulled around to the back of the building. The parking lot was filled with big holes because most of the red gravel had washed away a long time ago. Cornell parked the 1956 Chevy truck we were riding in next to the building and we got out and went inside.

Alvi was behind the bar doing paper work but he stopped, looked up, smiled at us and said, "Heah guys, can I offer you something to drink while I finish my paperwork? Then we can talk about the equipment." Cornell said, "Yeah man, do you have a couple of cold Miller Lite quarts?" Alvi slid the door back on the beer cooler that sat under the counter, grabbed two quarts of beer and put them on the bar counter top. He reached on the shelf behind him and got three beer glasses and sat them beside the quarts. I grabbed the beer, Sam and Cornell grabbed the glasses and we went to find a booth to sit down in. Beer was our morning drink of choice ... no orange juice for us. For the record, it was our noon and night choice too and we never missed an opportunity to drink it ... especially when it was free.

Now Alvi's Place was not a large club. Kitchen, bar, dance floor, restrooms, jukebox and all were enclosed in a space less that 950 sq ft. But for the residents of Oakland, Tennessee it was Las Vegas. While we were waiting for Alvi to finish his work I went over to the jukebox to see what songs was on it. There was some Johnny Taylor, Bobby Blue Bland, B.B. King, Al Green, Little Milton and the other mixture of R&B and Blues artists' songs. As I looked down the Al Green list I saw the song that I had played the drum track on when it was recorded. I put my quarter in the jukebox and punched the play button. The song, *To Sir With Love,* started playing and Al's unique voice, the song's melody and my funky beat filled the small club. A lot of people didn't know it but at one time Al Green had a large ranch in Oakland, Tennessee not very far from Alvi's nightclub. He gave it up and a lot of other things too after a girlfriend named Mary Woodson assaulted him by dousing him with grits before killing herself at Al's Memphis home on October 18, 1974.

Cornell had called Alvi earlier in the week. He and Sam knew Alvi because they had family and friends that lived out there in Oakland and they had spent a big part of their lives growing up there shooting craps, stealing, and making and drinking moonshine until they got shipped away in their teens to the Gary Job Corps Center a few miles east of San Marco, Texas. Cornell had later spent time in the Navy perfecting the skills that he had developed in Oakland.

Alvi finished his paper work and came and sat down in the booth. As I mentioned earlier, we had spent the concert deposit and didn't have any money to pay a rental fee until later so Cornell began to plead our 'pay you later' case for the rental of the equipment to Alvi. He said, "Alvi man, if you let us rent your equipment you can make some money and we can make some money. We'll have it back here way before you need it tonight. We promise man. We'll even throw in a free concert for you."

Stumbling Over A Quarter To Pick Up A Penny

Alvi was hesitant to rent us the equipment ... probably because he knew Cornell's and Sam's past schemes. But he looked at me and had just heard me playing drums on Al's song and maybe that gave legitimacy to our argument because I could see him beginning to lean our way ... and I knew that we had struck again.

At that moment the front door, which was about 30 feet away, opened and in walked John Butler. As he walked toward the bar a sour stench filled the room and you could see an evil yellow cloudy tint in his eyes. Alvi looked at us and said, "Excuse me. I'll be right back." He got up and went behind the bar that was about 25 feet to the left of where we were sitting to talk to John. As another song starting playing, Johnny Taylor's *Disco Lady,* Cornell, Sam and I winked at each other and started discussing how we would complete this deal and wrap up the concert later in the day.

In the background we could hear Alvi and John talking over the music. The discussion started off quiet but quickly got heated. I heard Alvi say, "You can't have it until you give me what you owe me." There was a couple of seconds of silence and I heard Alvi say, "No, don't...." Then I heard what sounded like a big firecracker exploding. As I looked up I heard the front door slam. I couldn't see Alvi anymore and John was gone too. Cornell got up and raced around behind the bar and found Alvi lying on his back in an ever-growing pool of blood. Cornell used his Navy training and applied pressure to the gunshot wound but he couldn't stop the bleeding and as Sam and I stood there and watched, Alvi took his last breath and died.

This was the first person that I had seen die violently and it had an enormous impact on my life. All of my pre-med biology courses had not prepared me for this. Cutting up cats, rabbits and sharks in an anatomy lab was just not the same. As I knelt over Alvi's body, I couldn't get over how his blood looked when it puddled on top of the dusty brown concrete floor less than two feet away.

There were several details that were tragic about this story. One of them was that John suffered from schizophrenia and shouldn't have been out on the streets. He should have been at the Tennessee state mental hospital up the highway in Bolivar or at the one in Memphis. He had pawned a pistol to Alvi several weeks ago for $50 and had come by last night to get his gun. He hadn't had Alvi's money and Alvi wouldn't give him the gun. John had left, but some people who were there that night later told the police that John had threatened Alvi. They said that John had told Alvi, "You better have my gun tomorrow or else." Evidently Alvi had heard these kinds of threats before and had taken this one as a hollow threat too. But on that day John followed through on his threat and Alvi had called the wrong bluff. He had called a crazy man's bluff and it didn't work out in his favor.

It took the rest of the morning to discuss what had happened with the Oakland police. Here we were again with the police. We would always be stopped by the cops every Friday, every Saturday, every Sunday ... every day of the week. Daytime or nighttime it didn't matter. They would never arrest us but they would certainly harass us. Looking back on those times we probably needed it.

Cornell, Sam and I would always have 2 or 3 schemes working and almost all of them were illegal or bordered on being illegal. After the police were finished with us that morning we put the equipment in the back of the truck and went to the concert. We figured that we had to at least show up. When we got there Cornell got on the stage and said, "We are going to have to cancel the concert today because a person who is instrumental to the concert's success, Alvi, died this morning at his club in Oakland in a senseless killing. Please bow your heads with us as we say a prayer for him and his family." He said "Father God ... we don't know the purpose or the reasons for the things that You do in our lives and those who You allow for us to come into contact with each day. We do however believe in Your Sovereign power and we will continue to try to do Your Will. We ask for Your blessings for Alvi's family. We ask that You lift them up right now like only you can. And father we ask that you bless this Holly Springs Motorcycle Club celebration and protect them and their family from all hurt, harm and danger. In Jesus name we pray. Amen."

When Cornell finished praying there wasn't a dry eye out there and through that prayer we not only turned the live concert into a memorial for Alvi where a deejay played records ... but the concert deposit was designated as a gift to the family and additional money was collected for a tribute to Alvi and his family. Whether or not the money got to Alvi's family, I don't know. I do know that Alvi's Place over on Highway 64 in Oakland never opened again as a nightclub and that we never gave Alvi the free concert that we had promised either.

Stumbling Over A Quarter To Pick Up A Penny

Shortly after this tragedy happened I stopped hanging around with Cornell and Sam. It was at this time, when I was as deep into **Servitude** as I could go, that God compelled me to change my behavior, get some new associates and return to using constructive habits. And you know what happened? God allowed my slide into **Servitude** to end and I started to rid myself of my self-destructive habits.

Looking back over that day, if John had come in just shooting at random it could have been me who was shot because when Alvi came to sit with us in the booth he sat down right beside me. The Bible says in Romans 7:15, "For what I am doing, I do not understand. For what I will to do, that I do not practice; but what I hate, that I do." If I had known this scripture I'm convinced that what was happening to me back then would have made more sense ... because while the schemes and the situations that I found myself participating in were exciting to me I really hated participating in them. I got no satisfaction from taking advantage of individuals' trust when we manipulated them with our schemes. I no longer enjoyed being around the people who I was doing the schemes with ... but I didn't see a way out.

Let's talk for a minute about **Servitude** *... we'll call it* **Letting Satan Set Your Agenda.**

Are You Letting Satan Set Your Agenda?

You are in **Servitude** when God's **Power** has been replaced by Satan's purpose in your life. You've gotten there after spending some time of your life in **Decline**. The Greek would say: "You have a serious lack of enkrateia. Enkrateia isn't a vitamin; it's a virtue." Today we call it self-control. Like Cornell, Sam and me in the story above ... you tell lies and devise and implement schemes that you want to use to empower yourself with but actually when they are completed they keep you in **Servitude**. Remember this ... **an ignorance of God's sovereign authority coupled with a lack of self-control and self-discipline will lessen the morals that you use to benchmark your actions and you will be kept in Servitude.** A lack of self-control leaves you venerable to Satan's plans for you ... and you allow him to set your agenda. As Paul said o in Romans 7:15, "... but what I hate, that I do." These words ring true for me back in 1979 and the story above was just one of many situations that I found myself in back then when God wanted me to take the steps to move back into His **Power** but Satan had me trapped in **Servitude.**

What's your story? Let's look further and see if you can find it.

The more trouble that you are in, the bigger the lie that you have to tell to get out of it.

When in **Servitude** you'll lie and scheme about anything and everything ... anybody and everybody ... anytime that it is convenient for you. You even use God in your schemes because you have long since stopped fearing Him ... that happened when you were in **Decline**. The Bible says in Psalms 14:1, "The fool *(one who is morally deficient)* says in his heart, 'There is no God.' They are corrupt, their deeds are vile; there is no one who does good." (emphasis added) So you find yourself trapped in **Servitude** to your lies, your schemes and your behavior or the lies, and schemes and behavior of those who you are associating with. Being in **Servitude** you constantly find yourself in places that can get you killed spiritually if not physically. Believe me, I know.

You enter into a Servitude period in your life when you don't take the right steps to end your Decline period.

Being in **Servitude** is the result of wrong choices you make. As in my story above, not only does being in **Servitude** impact you, but it also endangers everyone that comes into contact with you. In the above story Cornell, Sam and I were in **Servitude** to our greed, stupidity, ignorance, and arrogance and were just picking up pennies. By distracting Alvi that morning we very well could have been responsible for him being off guard when John showed up and killed him. While we know that his death was under the sovereign Will of God and that John was just an instrument of God's Will, we probably wouldn't have been there if we were not in **Servitude** and had been some other place picking up quarters and not stumbling over them.

So how do you get out of Servitude?

First, you need to determine if you are in **Servitude.** In the Bible, **Servitude** always comes after **Decline.** Whenever the Children of Israel started to engage in immoral and improper behavior they soon slid into **Decline.** Once they began to let Satan set their agenda they fell into **Servitude.** Their actions became contrary to the nature, character and Will of God ... in other words they began to sin and stayed in sin until they repented. Today the same is true. You may be in **Servitude** if you are engaging in any number of sinful activities including participating in perverse sexual behavior, using illicit drugs, overindulging in the use of alcoholic, gossiping, lying, stealing, gambling and the list goes on and on and on.

To get out of **Servitude** you must go through a **Probation** period. Satan would have you to take a different path, an easier path; one that would leave you unprepared to function in life other than in a position of **Servitude** or **Decline.** If Satan can get you to ignore Probation and take the actions appropriate for one of the other five periods he can keep you in **Servitude** because you will not have dealt properly with the *spoils* of **Servitude** ... the perverse sexual behavior, the use of illicit drugs, the overindulgence in alcoholic, the gossiping, the lying, the stealing, the gambling and the other ungodly behavior that caused you to be in your situation in the first place. Are you in **Servitude**?

You are in Servitude when you allow Satan to use people or your bad habits to continuously detach, distract or distance you from God.

In Servitude you permit Satan to set your agenda by allowing him to control your thoughts and actions. You are struggling and probably unaware of it. But the struggle doesn't have to end with Satan still in control of your agenda. Think about it. Even though you are struggling you still have all of the power that God has ever placed in you ... you just need to know how to reactivate it.

How do you reactivate your power?

A Prison Without Walls

I found that being in **Servitude** is similar to being in a *prison without walls*. You know, like the glamour slammers for the rich where they stay put on their own without guards until they serve out their sentence. They stay there letting someone else tell them what to do while they just plan what they will do once they are released on probation. Once they get on probation they undergo preparation to re-enter society. Just like many of you who find yourself in your daily life of *prison without walls*, your path out of **Servitude** is through **Probation**. It's the path that God uses to reactivate His **Power** in you.

The transformation of Apostle Paul is a really good example of a man being in **Servitude** and finding his way to God's **Power** through **Probation** and **Conquest**. Paul had been in **Servitude** to Satan when he was persecuting the early Christians. He was letting Satan set his agenda. The Bible says, when he was converted on the road to Damascus, Jesus sent him to be with Ananias so that he could teach him about being a Christian. Jesus knew that Paul was already an Old Testament scholar and that he needed to be placed in **Probation** until he acquired the strength of the Gospel necessary for him to move into **Conquest**. While on **Probation** with Ananias, in that *prison without walls,* he was able to first remove the errant habits that he had acquired through years of improper training and later prepare for future conquests. There in **Probation** he reactivated his power to accomplish a different purpose ... one that had nothing to do with Satan's agenda. In other words he went from **Servitude** into **Probation** and through **Preparation** before beginning **Conquest** and eventually moving into God's **Power**. It was there in **Probation** with Ananias that he learned that in order ...

To start removing yourself from Servitude you need to stop letting Satan set your agenda.

Those Good Old Memories

On the day that Paul stopped letting Satan set his agenda God immediately reactivated His **Power** in Paul and designated it to be used for a different purpose ... a Godly purpose. Notice that Paul didn't need to retreat to a better time and place. In life sometimes we try to retreat to a better time and place and it's that retreating rather than moving forward that causes us to fall out of God's **Power** and wind up in **Decline** and **Servitude** periods. You see, God knows that we all have *good memories* of supposedly better times and places and that we will try to return to those periods in our life to find refuge when we don't understand the current events that are happening in our life. But God wants us to retreat to Him and when we don't we create problems for ourselves.

Remember that g*ood memories* are relative and what was great, say twenty years ago, isn't so outstanding today. We disappoint ourselves all of the time by retreating to *good memories* instead of focusing our energy on conquering our next challenge. Think about it ... if you are a Baby Boomer the music from the 1970s sounds as good today as it did back then ... but you just won't look quite as cool now as you did back then wearing that mini-skirt, afro and those peace signs no matter what your *good memories* are.

Looking back now over my **Servitude** periods, I see that I needed to do what the scripture says in James 4:7, "Submit yourselves, then, to God. Resist the devil, and he will flee from you." In other words, I needed to surrender to God's Sovereign Will and stop letting Satan set my agenda.

While most of the time the way to reactivate God's **Power** in you is to allow Him to move you from **Servitude** into **Probation** and then to **Preparation, Conquest** and finally back to **Power** ... but sometimes you don't have to go through **Probation** to get back to God's **Power**. You can do as Nehemiah did when God put it on his heart to rebuild the walls of Jerusalem. He prayed, planned and got busy. You must say, "Let's see what God has in store for me. Let's pick up the quarter and not the penny" and then let God move you into **Preparation** so that He can use you. No matter how long or deep you have been in **Servitude** when God wants you back in His **Power** He will establish a retreat for you, a place for you to be restored, just as He did for Paul. I know He will do it because the

Bible says "Many are the plans in a man's heart, but it is the LORD's purpose that prevails." (Proverbs 19:21)

During my **Servitude** period described previously, "the bigger the problem, the bigger the lie" ... that was how I operated. As I later found out the truth was that the bigger the lie, the bigger the problem I created for myself by telling it and the further I fell into **Servitude**. I was ***Stumbling Over A Quarter To Pick Up A Penny*** and still not taking the actions that would allow me to take the least difficult path of **Preparation** back to God's **Power**.

When in **Servitude** you must find a place to be restored like Jerusalem, a city where even though it was destroyed many times it was always rebuilt. You need a stronghold like that where you can prepare yourself for new challenges and worship God too. Your Jerusalem must be your refuge and even though the walls might get torn down sometimes you can still go back there and rebuild your city of refuge and its walls just as Ezra, Zerubbabel, and Nehemiah did after the Babylonian captivity. It will be your place of **Preparation**. It will be the place where you throw out the bad habits from your past and learn to become blameless. But if you don't throw out the bad habits and rebuild ... and if you don't make the right changes ... you'll stay in **Servitude**.

During this time I was locked into a fool's way of life and became reticent so God decided that I wasn't ready to take the shortest path of **Preparation** back to His Power like Ezra, Zerubbabel, and Nehemiah did ... so He put me on **Probation**.

Chapter Three
Probation: The Psychic Plowboys Experience

A Psychic Plowboy Experience occurs for me when God still blesses me and allows me to make my way back to His **Power** when I do something for the wrong reason or stay in a situation longer than I should. He puts me on **Probation** and I have to work my way out of the situation and back to the place where He intended for me to be. Academia calls the type of behavior I described above as *duplicity* and the Bible calls it being *double-minded* ... but calling it a Psychic Plowboy Experience works better for me.

Forty And Double-minded

Some men at forty years old buy a red corvette, have an affair, do some other dumb thing and then come back to their senses and get on with life. Not me. Since I had already exhibited a lifetime of bad behavior (doing dumb things) by the late seventies, what I did in the early nineties when I turned forty-years old was to retire from my Senior Software Engineer position at the Dover Elevator Company in Horn Lake, Mississippi, get a Commercial and Industrial building contractor's license, spend $ 3,000 on a new drum set and then set out to revive the Psychic Plowboys ... a mid-1980s locally popular punk rock 'n' roll band. Although it had been years since I had heard from my scheming buddies Cornell and Sam I hadn't completely given up scheming yet and had developed a plan to use the Psychic Plowboys to make me rich. My thoughts were that since rock 'n' roll purchases amounted to 65 - 70% of all music purchases, if the band could develop a hit CD I could put my hands deep into the pocket of parents all over the world who supplied the money to their teenagers to buy rock 'n' roll music. If we could create a sizeable teenage Psychic Plowboys fan base then their parents would provide the money for us to keep their children's habit going ... and

Stumbling Over A Quarter To Pick Up A Penny

those teenagers would make me rich and provide me the mailbox money to keep me rich for years to come.

I almost pulled it off too but I double-crossed myself. I was telling myself that the reason that I was reestablishing the band was to get rich but actually it was for something else. Double-crossing yourself on reasons for your behavior is quite common when you are in **Probation** like I was during this time. You ask yourself, "Am I good or am I bad? Is what I'm doing good or is it bad?" You really don't know ... because after all, you are on **Probation** because of some former bad behavior. You are struggling to control the **Servitude** period tendencies to lie and exhibit all of the other poor moral behavior that is still inside of you.

I was really stumbling at that time but I didn't have a clue that I was ... so I double-crossed myself and convinced myself that I was re-starting the band in order to pick up some quarters and get rich ... but all the time I knew that I just wanted to have some fun picking up pennies like I did when I was scheming several years ago.

Thinking about the great times that I had had and the easy money that I had made playing music in the seventies was the mindset that I was in when I sold the plan to resurrect the Psychic Plowboys to Dave Blair and Eric Phillips. We were sitting in Zinnie's Restaurant that was located on the northeast corner of Madison Avenue and N. Belvedere Boulevard in Midtown Memphis drinking draft beer. It was the winter of 1993. I had met Dave at the Dover Elevator Company where we both worked in the engineering department. Dave knew Eric from playing music together in the mid-1980s. I said, "Dave, didn't you play with a band that was pretty well known around town in the mid and late eighties?" Dave said, "Yeah, me and Eric had this band called the Psychic Plowboys, we were in all of the local papers, music magazines and we sold out all of the local venues we played in?" I said, "Wow! Why did you split up?" "One of the band members became too much of a hassle to deal with." Eric said. I said, "What do you think about starting the band back up". Dave and Eric looked at each other, smiled and Dave said, "Why not?" We shook hands in agreement and that night set a goal to have a CD completed and ready for release by the beginning of the summer in 1994.

So we formed a business called Global Concerns Limited and set up shop on the second floor of a two-story warehouse building directly across the street from the Loraine Motel where Dr. Martin Luther King Jr. was killed in 1968. It is the same motel that now houses The National Civil Rights Museum. Our building was located on the northwest corner of Huling Street and Mulberry Street in the South Main District of downtown. We turned the space into a loft and built in a kitchen, bathroom, bedrooms and a sound stage to practice in and record the live CD.

The band was supposed to have four members. Dave would play lead and rhythm guitar and Eric would play bass guitar. I played drums so all we needed was a lead singer. After auditioning several individuals to be the lead singer, and against strong objection from Eric, we settled on Dan Hopper who had been the problem band member that Eric had mentioned when we had met earlier that winter. The Rev. Doctor Daniel Morrison Hopper III was Dan's stage name. After meeting him, initially I couldn't understand why Eric was so vehemently opposed to the person that everyone called 'Big Dan' being in the band ... but it wasn't long before I got the picture.

Dan was an alcoholic. We had found him working at a pizza shop in East Memphis. He was living with his parents off of Ridgeway Road also in East Memphis. In hindsight we should have left him there twirling pizzas and crying in his beer about how life had been so unfair to him. But at that time, while he couldn't sing and screamed most of his lyrics, he did fit the bill for the unforgettable front man that we needed. He was the kind of front man that would say anything and do anything that we told him to do. Unfortunately he did lots of things that we didn't tell him to do too.

We got the ball rolling and recorded the Psychic Plowboys CD live on March 25 at the world famous punk rock Antenna Club on Madison a block west of Zinnie's. We then began to take advantage of some of the contacts that the band had previously made. One of those contacts was James Manning, a Kentucky native, who was the manager at the New Daisy Club on Beale Street. James was also the music page editor of a local music paper The Memphis Flyer. James was a greasy-haired near-hillbilly who, although in his early thirties, loved rap music. It was James who introduced us to Nicolas Veltman, a Dutch student who was studying the music of the Mid-South at Ole Miss in Oxford, Mississippi. Nicolas booked the band on a six-week European concert tour. And while the tour was fun several incidents that happened on it led to the band disbanding when we got back to Memphis.

During this yearlong Psychic Plowboys Experience I spent several thousand dollars of my money and hundreds of hours of my time. I see now that it was the tool that God used to get me to move to a **Preparation** period in my life. The six-week European concert tour in 1995, just like my homeless period in the seventies, was when God broke several of my dependencies that were preventing me from moving to the place where he wanted me to go.

Now the whole Physic Plowboys story is a book by itself. I just used some of it because it helped me to clearly identify one of my **Probation** periods. It is a really good example of how I wound up in Probation by doing the absolute wrong things for the wrong reasons ... I now see that I wasn't really trying to get rich but rather my imagination was trying to relive a past that I remembered to be great that wasn't really that great at all. My father, quoting Abraham Lincoln, had once told me, "Hayward, 'there is no lesson to be learned from the second kick of a mule'" ... and I hadn't learned that lesson yet.

*Let's take a minute to examine the **Probation** period.*

You'll enter a Probation period if you allow yourself to compare your present achievements incorrectly against your past accomplishments.

Prior to the Psychic Plowboys commitment I was frustrated with my achievements ... a condition that a lot of forty-year olds find themselves in. I don't know why I felt that way. Actually, life was going really well for me. I had come through the late eighties and early nineties expanding in **Conquest** and flourishing in God's **Power**. But at forty years old I hit a brick wall. I was probably frustrated because unknowingly I was accepting the media's agenda that creates continuous personal dissatisfaction and constant need and I was ripe to fall for anything that came along. I was raising two children with their mother and in addition to my job at the Dover Elevator Company I had a thriving tax preparation business. I had built a custom $250,000 dollar house for my family to live in and I owned property in several other areas of the city including a vacant lot up the street from our home where I planned on building a spec house.

Even with all of these successes I was frustrated and I couldn't see what was wrong in my life. But now I know that I was frustrated because my habits had become so terrible that they provided me with almost no positive experiences in my life. I had turned my back on God and even though my wife invited me to attend church with her, and I knew that I should go, I wasn't attending regularly and when I did go my being there didn't really mean anything to me. As the Bible says in James 1:8, "[I] was a double-minded man and unstable" in all that I did. I was in a **Probation** period and was making poor decisions that were not based on God's plan for me and my family. So, without God's **Power** in my life and no positive reference point to benchmark the blessings and favor that God was granting me, I turned my back on Him and made the kind of Psychic Plowboys Experience decision that moves you deeper into **Probation.**

How Are Your Habits?

You will find yourself in a Probation period when God is trying to get your attention to tell you that you need to make changes in your life.

Being in **Probation** has little to do with how much money, wealth or localized power you have acquired. You know what it has to do with? Habits. Og Mandino wrote in his book, *The Greatest Secret in the World*, "As a child I was [a] slave to my impulses; now I am a slave to my habits, as are all grown men."[1] What does that mean to you and me? It means that when we were children our parents or some other authority figure controlled our actions but when we become adults we are controlled by our habits. If we have good habits, more often than not, we are successful and will spend a majority of our time in God's **Power**. If we don't have good habits we will spend most of our time in **Probation**, **Decline** or **Servitude.** Take a minute to think about those who you know are successful. What kinds of habits do they have? Do they read the word of God regularly, give hilariously and take action on their ideas and dreams? Do they work with God and not against Him?

While I was in this **Probation** period God showed me that I could change my life, remove myself from a less than positive situation and not hurt the relationship that I had with my children, Chip and Dorian. This experience actually allowed me the opportunity to work with God and let Him winnow out most of the bad habits I had acquired since the early eighties. I also was able to get rid of the most of the *spoils* that I had held onto from my battles in the seventies.

I stayed in this **Probation** period for almost three years until God felt that I was prepared enough to move on. During this time I didn't own a television and I read a lot. I got into the best physical shape of my life but I still made one big mistake ... I didn't get back into Christ's church.

Let me ask you some questions: Are your habits what they need to be to sustain you? Are there any habits that you need to get rid of? Then what are you waiting on? When you subdue one bad habit the next one is overcome with less of a struggle. All you have to do is to ... **confess your sins and start making the right decisions for the right reasons.**

The effort that I put into the Psychic Plowboys didn't make me rich like I had planned. But I did make decent money with my construction company during this time and looking back if I had devoted the time and energy to my construction company that I had done to the Psychic Plowboys I would probably have tripled my investment. But I was greedy and wanted instant wealth and that was a problem for me. If I had known what the Bible says in Proverbs 15:27, "A greedy man brings trouble to his family ..." then those three years that I spent in **Probation** during that time could have possibly been "3 months or 3 days or 3 minutes long" ... but I was ***Stumbling Over A Quarter To Pick Up A Penny*** so I needed the entire 3 years to get right.

My stumbling led me to become depraved when all I really had to do to get upright was to confess my sins and get on with God's work. But I was in this Psychic Plowboy induced **Probation** period and when I figured out what was happening I had squandered most of my wealth and all I had left was a little wisdom. It was here where God reminded me of one of my **Preparation** periods. Let's see what that **Preparation** period looked like.

Chapter Four

Preparation: Baby Eagles and Piano Lessons

On most Saturday mornings my father would drop my older brother, three sisters and me off at Ms. E. O. Miller's house, that's Ethel Ophelia Miller, for piano lessons. She taught a 5th grade class at our school and on weekends she taught piano lessons and baby eagles how to fly.

Our school, Geeter, was a 1st through 12th grade county school. It was the oldest school for African-Americans in rural Shelby County and it was located southwest of the Memphis city limits. My family lived about two miles northeast of the school on a portion of 300 acres of land that had been owned by our family for decades. My dad had built our house on a 1.5 acre lot there soon after my second oldest sister Marion was born in the early 1950s. There were six children in our family; my brother Joe Jr., was the oldest. The three girls: Mamie, Marion and Carol were born next, in that order. Then I came and finally, in 1959, my brother Rick, the third boy and sixth child, was born.

Now Ms. Miller lived in Midtown Memphis with other African-American professionals in the area around South Parkway East and South Bellevue (now called Elvis Presley Blvd). It took my dad about fifteen minutes to drive the ten miles to her quaint little four-room house on James Street, the third parallel street west of South Bellevue. Her house was located on the east side of the street that ran north and south between South Parkway East and Kerr Avenue. It was a happy little house with an effeminate touch to it. It had been built in the 1940s and had an elevated front porch and a small backyard.

Ms. Miller was a strict disciplinarian. She taught baby eagles how to fly using guided-experience. My parents knew that for their baby eagles to fly, to be successful, we needed not just experience but guided-experience ... the kind of experience that contained wisdom for future use. They knew that we needed as much access to that kind of experience as possible so that we would learn how to submit ourselves to those who were wise and be open to their authority. They knew that if we learned to submit to the authority of man in our youth we would be prepared to learn and understand the wisdom of submitting to God's authority in adulthood. The Bible says in 1 Peter 5:5-6, "Likewise you younger people, submit yourselves to *your* elders. Yes, all of *you* be submissive to one another, and be clothed with humility, for "God resists the proud, but gives grace to the humble." Therefore humble yourselves under the mighty hand of God, that He may exalt you in due time...."

Ms. Miller provided us some of that guided-experience. Contained in the preparation that we received from her was the wisdom that we would need to successfully transition from being a young inexperienced apprentice in our youth to seasoned journeymen as we grew older. I remember that she taught me simple things like how to use proper manners and how to respect others when I was in her classroom during the week. While at her house on the weekends she taught me how to be open to reproof ... and for me that was tough. Ms. Miller, one of God's choices to assist in my **Preparation**, was a very unique person to me. I thank God for placing her in my life.

As far as the actual piano lessons went, my oldest sister Mamie was by far the most accomplished. She played a solo piece at her 8th grade graduation commencement exercise. I never became that good, though. I was nine years old and learning my basic chords when one day my father said, "Hayward, since you are always going around beating on everything do you want to learn how to play the drums?" I said, "Yes sir." So I started taking drum lessons and by the time I was ten years old I was playing in the high school band and by my early teens I was playing in the night clubs around Memphis, like Curry's Club Manhattan and Bill's Twilight Zone, with my older brother Joe's band.

My father through his action of noticing my percussive skills showed that he wasn't a selfish man but a wise father who was attentive to that individual gift that God had given me. By not forcing me to continue to learn to play the piano he allowed me to accept my personal gift from God and to develop a passion to play the drums. What he realized was that there was more than one way for music to impact my life and develop in me the discipline that he knew I would need in life. My father's actions were a perfect demonstration of Proverbs 22:6 which says, "Train a child in the way he should go, and when he is old he will not turn from it." For years this scripture has been misinterpreted. So what is the correct interpretation? It means that as a parent or leader we should observe unselfishly those that depend on us for guidance and take the time to help them develop their gifts based on what God has placed in them even if that is not what we wish for them to do.

My parents knew that baby eagles needed to learn how to fly. So that's why in addition to making sure that we went to church, completed our homework and finished our chores, on Saturday mornings dad would drive the 10 miles to take us to Ms. Miller's house for The Piano Lessons. I'm convinced that they believed, as a lot of African-American parents did at that time, that there were two undertakings that their children needed to do if they were to be upwardly mobile. Playing the piano was one and watching Lawrence Welk (ah one, ah two) was the other. Don't laugh. If you were an African-American child growing up during this time you had to watch Lawrence Welk too.

Evidently my parents knew in the 1960s that playing the piano or other musical instruments and listening to music from cultures other than our own would help to develop the neurons in our brains and increase our intelligence. I believe that they felt that playing a musical instrument would grow in us the discipline necessary to take on abstract challenges. I believe that they felt that it taught us that constant effort, no matter how small, if consistently undertaken and with proper instruction, could lead to accomplishments that we could be proud of. It worked ... I'm evidence that it worked and all of my sisters and brothers are evidence too.

Music lessons were not cheap and we took them year-round. I don't know how mom and dad afforded them especially in the wintertime when dad's masonry business was slow and he and his crew weren't working on many projects. My mother at that time was a homemaker and had never worked outside of the home so I'm sure that it was a financial struggle and a sacrifice for them to pay for the lessons but they knew what we needed and they were determined to prepare their baby eagles to fly. It was evident to them that our experiencing the discipline of learning to play the piano and through it acquiring other tools necessary to succeed in a rapidly changing world was worth the sacrifice.

Stumbling Over A Quarter To Pick Up A Penny

Taking these lessons was one of the many **Preparation** periods in my life that God had provided for me under the guidance of my parents and other trusted individuals. However, there was one situation that neither The Piano Lessons nor any of my other experiences had prepared me for when it happened ... and that was when my dad died.

When my father died of cancer in 1974 music and a lot of other stuff took a back seat in my life. Even though I stayed in college, **Preparation** was over for me. I moved into short-lived periods of **Conquest** and God's **Power** and then quickly began a downward spiral into **Decline**. My father had been the only person in my life who seemed to take the time to observe me, understand the pace that I moved at and accept what I saw for me in my life. He was quiet but strong. He never forced his way on you unless it was totally necessary and that was when he used his experience to help you make a better decision.

My dad used the guided-experience method to prepare eagle to fly too. In my **Preparation** he often used it when he showed me the wisdom of patience and planning. He used it when teaching others who were under his care. He told me a story about how he taught an anxious young apprentice crewmember how to approach a complicated masonry project. He had watched the apprentice's tendency of starting projects before properly planning for them. So he let the anxious young worker start building a wall without measuring the space properly and before developing a complete project plan. When the young worker got to the top of the wall and was almost finished he saw that in order to finish the job he would have to do some unsightly plugging of the remaining space or tear the wall down and redo it correctly. He asked my father, "Mr. Townsend, what should I do?" My dad answered his question by asking him, "Charles, what should you do to do the job right and for it to be something that you would be proud to show to your son in the future?" and Charles said, "I should tear it down, measure the space, create my plan and then do it right?" My dad said, "That's right ... but what else have you learned to take with you from now on about the importance of planning?" Charles said, "I learned that if I plan before I start I'll save myself a lot of time and effort."

I met this man, Charles Williams, in 1988 when he and his crew were doing the masonry work on the house that I was building for my family. I had contacted him through a mutual friend who highly recommended him for the job. When we started to talk I commented on how good his project near the University of Memphis looked. I had reviewed it before selecting him to do the work. As we continued to talk he started telling me about how he got started in the business. He told me that a man named Mr. Townsend had helped to prepare him to be successful over thirty years ago when he was a young anxious apprentice. "Was his name Joe Townsend and did he have a business partner name Mr. Gene Braden?" I said. He asked, "Yes, that's right. Did you know him?" I said, "Boy did I know him ... he was my father." And then I laughed and said, "I see that he taught you some of the same lessons that he taught me and my sisters and brothers." He then told me how much he appreciated not only what my father had taught him but how he had done it ... quietly and patiently ... providing him just the right preparation that specifically fitted his need ... not the general information that other men he had worked for gave to their crews. Charles today is a masonry journeyman and has run his own successful business since my dad retired in 1963. By the way, he did an excellent job on my house.

Except for going to church my dad practiced what he preached. I often remember seeing him sitting in his favorite chair planning before he started working on any project. His approach to completing tasks represented the perfect example of Luke 14:28-30 that says, "Suppose one of you wants to build a tower. Will he not first sit down and estimate the cost to see if he has enough money to complete it? For if he lays the foundation and is not able to finish it, everyone who sees it will ridicule him, saying, 'This fellow began to build and was not able to finish.'" I'm sure that's my organizational skills came from the methods that my father learned from that scripture. In fact, all of my sisters and brothers and even my children have some of the same organizational skills that my father used everyday in his business.

Dad and mom prepared us for life's challenges by setting strong examples and consistently enabling us to actively engage in actions that encouraged us to develop our gifts from God. The Piano Lessons was just one of the many guided-experiences that my parents prepared us with because they knew that ... **even the high soaring eagle has to at first be prepared and encouraged to fly.**

Let's talk about **Preparation.**

God allows you to be in Preparation when there is a gift or gifts that He wants you to develop or wisdom that He wants you to understand and take forward into future periods of Conquest and Power.

What Inheritance Are You Leaving?

As you will see later ... **you always need to be taking on and conquering new challenges to remain in Power.** You need to be aware that God is constantly preparing you everyday through His various sovereign methods to conquer those new challenges. The positive people and situations that God places in your life help to prepare you. The negative people and situations that He allows in your life are there to prepare you as well. Let's me ask you a question here that will stretch your thought: Can positive and negative experiences and situations be considered as inheritance? I think so. Here's what I think. If the experiences passed to you are *your parent's or grandparent's experiences* then they are inheritance for you and your children. If the experiences are *your experiences* then they are inheritance to be passed to your children, grand children or others who God places under your care. That's why God wants those experiences passed on so that all of us are prepared to conquer the new challenges that are necessary to keep us in His **Power**. Proverbs 13:22 says, "A good man leaves an inheritance for his children's children, but a sinner's wealth is stored up for the righteous." The inheritance that my parents and grandparents left me wasn't unlimited assets but a wealth of wisdom, common sense and a preparedness to work through and conquer life's challenges. When we don't pass on the stories of our experiences we neglect to pass on our wealth.

Take a minute to think about periods of **Preparation** in your life. What inheritance was left for you? What inheritance are you leaving? Are you squandering that inheritance or are you using it wisely?

Taught Any Eagles How To Fly Lately?

God has always placed the responsibility on parents to nurture, educate and discipline their children. The Bible says in Acts: 7:20-21 that after Moses, a Hebrew and one of the God's greatest leaders in the Bible, was adopted by Pharaoh's daughter that she immediately began to prepare him for a proper life in Pharaoh's Egyptian court. In his biography on Moses, Chuck Swindoll writes that because Pharaoh had no son and heir, Moses was being nurtured for the throne. Consider these two verses:

> He was born; ... he was nurtured three months in his father's home. After he was exposed, [Pharaoh's] daughter took him away and nurtured him as her own son. (Acts 7:20-21)

The word nurture means *to rear, to educate, to train*. Pharaoh's daughter put Moses through the training of an Egyptian home, a wholly different proposition from a Hebrew home. Moses, being reared in Egypt with a silver spoon in his mouth, attended the Temple of the Sun, called by some the "Oxford of the ancient world".[2] Pharaoh's daughter assumed that her nurturing of Moses was to prepare him for the Egyptian throne. Boy, was she ever wrong. What were you nurtured for? What conquests has God been preparing you for?

Flying and Going Nowhere Fast

By the time I turned 16 years old my parents had followed God's instruction to nurture me. They had prepared me for my first adult **Conquest** period but I didn't know it. They had made sure that God's gifts in me had been initially developed and even though I had not learned how to soar yet, I had learned how to fly ... so I'm sure that my parents felt that it was just a matter of time before I would be soaring with the best of them. I had good manners and my behavior showed a presence of wisdom; I was active in the church, doing well in school and a young leader in the community. With all of those good things going on in my life I didn't know that it was time for me to move out of **Preparation.** I didn't know that I couldn't stay in **Preparation** forever ... I didn't know that it was time for me leave the nest and fly and then soar. If I had known the following scripture I would have realized that I was prepared and ready to move into **Conquest.** What scripture? The scripture in Proverbs 3:21-24 that says, "Dear friend, guard Clear Thinking and Common Sense with your life; don't for a minute lose sight of them. They'll keep your soul alive and well, they'll keep you fit and attractive. You'll travel safely; you'll neither tire nor trip. You'll take afternoon naps without a worry; you'll enjoy a good night's sleep. No need to panic over alarms or surprises, or predictions that doomsday's just around the corner, because GOD will be right there with you; he'll keep you safe and sound."

So when is it time to move out of Preparation? It's time when you have learned to fly a little bit ... and that is ... when you have learned to pray to God for direction, discipline and discernment ... and when you are able to conquer the challenges in front of you without being hindered by a stumbling spirit. When you are able to lie down in sweet sleep and not be afraid ... that's when you know that God has prepared you for His work and that it's time for you to move from **Preparation** into **Conquest**. In **Conquest**, when tests come, if you are prepared properly, your sound judgment will tell you that if the test is there to trip you up then it a test from Satan; but if the test is there to make you stand strong then you know that it is from a God who delights in your victories and has prepared you since your birth to succeed.

Let's see ... we've discussed **Decline, Servitude, Probation** and **Preparation.** ... *Let's now discuss* ***Conquest.***

Chapter Five

Conquest: Can You Hold Your Breath?

Hold your breath for three seconds before you read on.

If you held your breath ... let's say that you just extended control over your carnal nature. If you didn't ... let's say that you allowed your carnality to control you.

During my homeless time, in the middle and late 1970s, I didn't hold my breath on a lot of moral issues and my carnality reigned supreme in my life. But just a few years earlier, in the fall of 1972 until the summer of 1975, I had come out of **Preparation** and I had been able to hold my breath – control my carnality – and by doing so I had experienced the first real **Conquest** period in my adult life. I had completed my course requirements for medical school and was traveling around the world playing music. I was living in my own condominium. I was in my early twenties and I was living the really good life.

I would understand much later that God had been ready for me to move into **Power** after this **Conquest** period but I had turned my back on Him and couldn't see it. Instead I quickly moved through the **Power** period that I had been prepared for and went right into **Decline**. There are several reasons why I couldn't see God's plan for me. The following story is part of one of them.

I was a Memphis musician in the 1970s and everything was *free* for me: free drugs, free liquor, free sex and practically anything else you could imagine. At that time I often said to myself, "... it just didn't get much better than what I got going on." The band that I was the drummer for, Koheshun, was doing well. We hadn't released any recordings but that didn't prevent us from performing constantly at the same venues where Al Greene, Isaac Hayes, Confunshun, the Bar Kays, and other music industry R&B chart-toppers regularly played. Some of the local places like the Club Rosewood on S. Lauderdale, a converted movie theatre, stayed packed every night with live entertainment and I hung out there drinking and prowling when my band wasn't playing a concert somewhere. The Brooks Brothers Family Affair Club, just off of Vance Street in the Medical district, was a local hot spot too. Performing there and at the other nightclubs was like getting paid to be at a continuous party.

My plan had been to tour the world and play music for a couple more years until I got accepted into the Memphis-based Southern College of Optometry. There I would become an Ophthalmologist and specialize in diagnosing and treating diseases and injuries of the eye. These years were part of an extended **Conquest** and brief **Power** period for me and I flourished. In the beginning of this period I had worked everyday from "sun up to sun up" accomplishing goals and preparing myself for whatever was intended for me in my seemingly unlimited future. Most of the time during this period, in addition to playing with my band, I was a full time student at Memphis State and held two part time jobs.

I had an enormous amount of energy and applied it to the unlimited possibilities that were available to me now that segregation had "officially" ended and the U.S. Supreme court had caused Jim Crow to "fly the coop". I learned new skills and refined the older ones that I had gotten in my **Preparation** period. I took advantage of being in the music scene and played with every kind of band that I could ... from Gospel to Country & Western, from Hillbilly to Jazz, from Rock & Roll to R & B. With Memphis holding its place as the Music Capital of the South and money flowing in from every corner of the globe, it is easy to see how I got caught up in the music industry's *free* whirlwind lifestyle and went along for the ride.

In early 1975, I still hadn't had my first adult **Decline** and **Servitude** periods ... but they were on their way. I was still surviving off of the inheritance that my parents and grandparents had provided. Remember again as we read in the previous chapter on **Preparation** that the Bible says in Proverbs 13:22 that, "A good man leaves an inheritance for his children's children, but a sinner's wealth is stored up for the righteous." Back then I was like a lot of people today ... I was looking for my wealth but I wasn't righteous.

By mid-1975, the economic recession was well underway. I had squandered all of my wealth and all that I had left was a little wisdom and it wasn't of much value because at that time I didn't know that I had it. I had gone from being a motivated Management Intern in the Engineering Department at South Central Bell, the local telephone company at that time, to being a lazy parasite that lived off of credit cards. My part time job at the JCPenny warehouse had ended and I had used up the spiritual capital that God had invested in me through the guided-experience that people had given me. I had lost the goals and dreams that I once had for my life. I had become isolated, jaded and I lacked judgment. I didn't understand what Solomon meant when he wrote in Proverbs 24: 30-34, [I] "went past the field of the sluggard, past the vineyard of the man who lacks judgment; thorns had come up everywhere, the ground was covered with weeds, and the stone wall was in ruins. I applied my heart to what I observed and learned a lesson from what I saw: A little sleep, a little slumber, a little folding of the hands to rest and poverty will come on you like a bandit and scarcity like an armed man." If I had understood those verses I would have kept busy by making made a better effort to find legitimate work to do ... but I didn't.

In late 1975, after I had been living off of credit card purchases and cash advances for most of the year, I experienced the first two of many blows that I would experience over the next couple of years. One blow was the impact from the deepening of the economic recession that our country was in. It was being fueled by high energy prices and stagflation. The other blow, the knock out punch, was the drying up of the credit market that led to businesses scaling back their expansions while at the same time eliminating most of the available part-time jobs overnight ... including mine.

Those two blows were devastating and took a toll on me. They were followed by another blow brought on by the increased popularity of disco music and the demise of the black owned nightclubs and other venues that were geared toward live music performances. The relaxing of the Jim Crow laws helped to cause the failure of many of those black-owned businesses because their regular clientele could now go to integrated nightclubs and other venues that had previously been off-limits to them. More over, the nightclubs that survived could now make a profit by hiring a DJ rather than an expensive band. So, what little money I was making from playing music ended abruptly too.

Stumbling Over A Quarter To Pick Up A Penny

I found myself as a young man with no wealth, little wisdom and a whole lot of unanswered questions. I felt like I had nothing at all. I lost sight of God's sovereign **Power** and stopped using my gifts and talents to conquer new challenges. I realize now that this was the end of a **Conquest** period and the first time in my life when I started *Stumbling Over A Quarter To Pick Up A Penny.*

Here is what I learned about **Conquest**.

When you are in a Conquest period God is growing and expanding you so don't get lazy and stop identifying and using your gifts.

In the Bible a poor widow with two sons was told by the prophet Elisha to go and collect jars from her neighbors. The story in 2 Kings 4:1-7 says that when she asked him for help he replied and asked her, "Tell me, what do you have in your house?" "Your servant has nothing at all," she said, "except a little oil." He then told her to go and get not a few ... but a lot of empty jars from her neighbors. So she and her sons did as he said and when they came back home she shut the door and gathered the jars. She began to fill them from the *little oil* that she had and that *little oil* became *enough oil* to fill all of the jars that they had collected. She was pouring oil and adding to her wealth until she ran out of jars. Notice two things 1) She did not run out of oil ... she ran out of jars, and; 2) She almost didn't identify the oil as her wealth because it was just a *little bit of oil* ... but God saw it as enough to use to fill her jars until she ran out of them.

In the widow's story the *jar* is a symbol for gifts and the *oil* is a symbol for the wealth in God's **Power** that we can achieve by using them. What is your *oil*? How many jars have you collected in your life that sit empty? God doesn't want you to ever stop identifying and bringing your gifts *(jars)* to Him to be filled. The older you are the more jars you should have to bring if you've grown and expanded the gifts that He has given you and if you have made wise use of all of the preparation that He has sent your way.

Cracked Jars And A Little Bit Of Oil

When you are in a **Conquest** period you should bring jars in all situations and let God decide to stop filling them. Notice again that God only stopped filling the widow's jars when she ran out of jars. Some of the jars were probably old and cracked and some were probably new and unblemished. Their condition was not important to God ... He filled them anyway. If the widow and her sons had collected a hundred or a thousand more jars then I'm sure that the oil would have continued to flow when she poured it into them and her wealth would have continued to grow. Don't you make the decision to stop bringing jars because they may have cracks in them. God doesn't see the cracks in your jars ... only man sees them.

There's no need for you to *bring a jar* for God to fill if you are in Servitude because everything that you own will wind up under the control of the master that you are serving which is Satan.

If you are a drug addict the oil that goes into your jar will go to your master ... the drug man. If you are a whoremonger the oil that goes into your jar will end up under the control of your master ... the prostitute's pimp. If you are an addicted gambler ... you get the point. The Bible says in Proverbs 13:22, "...but a sinner's wealth is stored up for the righteous" and since the enemy will ultimately own your wealth why should God fill the jar that you bring?

Bringing *another jar* when you are in Decline won't work either.

God won't fill it because He knows that He would just be pouring oil into a jar that has a hidden crack in it that you are unaware of. God knows that even though He may ignore your crack and fill up your jar that it will soon be empty as the oil drains away unused. God knows that during this period you will be preoccupied with enjoying your bad habits and not ready from Him. He knows that you haven't realized what your *little bit of oil* is because your life has become empty.

Let's look at how King Solomon described his empty life in the Bible in the book of Ecclesiastes.

Although King Solomon built the Temple, achieved numerous political and intellectual accomplishments, and was the wisest and richest man in the known world, by the time he sat down to write Ecclesiastes his life was in **Decline** ... his jars had cracks in them and were just about empty. In the book he is saying, "don't be like me". I'm sure people were wondering, "Why would a king that has everything in his possession and has done so many things write those words?" What they didn't understand was that he was saying was, "Don't stop learning and conquering new ideas and redefining old ones. Don't become complacent in your life. Don't move away from God. Don't stop *bringing jars* ... even if they are cracked like mine are that's okay because God can ignore those cracks or fix them if he chooses." This brings up an important point. ... **It's not our responsibility to fix the cracks ... we just need to be obedient like the widow, bring the jars and then start pouring our "little bit" of oil in them.**

At the end of Solomon's reign God chose to not fill Solomon's jars or to ignore the cracks in them. So Solomon, with all of his wisdom and wealth ... guided-experience and other preparation was not spared the **Decline** period in life. When his jars finally emptied he died and the nation of Israel suffered. In many opinions, even to this day, the nation has still not recovered from Solomon's legacy. One thing to remember here is that those around you will suffer too when you are in **Decline**.

When you are in a Conquest period you can influence God if you are being obedient and righteous.

We can't change God's plan for us but we can influence Him. In the Bible in 2 Kings Chapter 20 is the story of Hezekiah who became King of Judah when he was twenty-five years old and reigned for twenty-nine years. He was a good and obedient and did what was right in God's eyes. From the beginning of his reign he lived in **Conquest**. He introduced religious reform and reinstated religious traditions. He removed the high places where other gods were worshipped. He smashed the sacred stones and cut down the Asherah poles that were used in idol worship. Late in his reign he became ill to the point of death and the prophet Isaiah told him to put his house in order because he would surely not recover and die. But Hezekiah humbled himself and prayed to God knowing that he had been obedient. He asked God to extend his life and was granted fifteen more years to live which he used to continue to add to the wealth of the nation of Israel.

> "Notwithstanding Hezekiah humbled himself for the pride of his heart, both he and the inhabitants of Jerusalem, so that the wrath of the LORD came not upon them in the days of Hezekiah." (2 Chronicles 32:26)

In our **Conquest** periods I believe we can influence God's sovereignty too if we are obedient like King Hezekiah was and if we continue to do what is good and right in God's eyes.

When you are in a **Conquest** period you really feel alive and never want to leave it. But if you've made good use of your time while you were there God will move you into an even better period called ... **Power**.

We've now covered five of the six periods, **Decline, Servitude, Probation, Preparation** and **Conquest.** *Now it's time to discuss* ***Power.***

Chapter Six
Power: Riding to the Games

By the time the mid-1990s came around I had conquered numerous challenges and without me knowing it God had moved me from a **Conquest** period to a period of **Power**. I had had some significant accomplishments so this **Power** period was different from the brief one that I experienced in the mid-1970s that I wrote about earlier in the first part of the chapter on **Conquest.**

My scheming days were over and I was regularly attending church. I had graduated from college with a degree in Mechanical Engineering and had spent several years as a Mechanical Design Supervisor and Senior Software Engineer in the manufacturing department at the Dover Elevator Company. I was serving on or had recently served on the board of directors of several national and international non-profit organizations. I was traveling around the world again ... Europe, the Caribbean and Africa. I was involved in Christian missions in the Republic of Senegal and the Republic of The Gambia in West Africa. I was very busy, always preoccupied and I didn't have time to think about the conquests that God was allowing me to have ... I just did them. I had gotten my life back on track. I was in God's Will and I flourished because I was in His **Power.**

When you are in God's Power good things automatically come into your life ... good mates, good friends and more opportunities than you know what to do with. It's like walking outside and finding the face of Benjamin Franklin on a one hundred dollar bill laying on the sidewalk in front of you just for the taking.

As I wrote earlier in the introduction, when you are in **Power**, people give you credit for doing good things that you didn't do. They also give you credit for being smarter than you may actually be. But I had learned not to be concerned about what people gave me credit for doing but to be concerned with what God would have me to do for Him.

I had learned my lesson and brought a lot of *jars* to God and He had faithfully filled them. He gave me joy and peace and purpose. He gave me physical and spiritual rewards. God knew that I still needed help so He placed a beautiful, intelligent and resourceful lady in my life and I married her, my wife Barbara, as soon as I could convince her to marry me. So over the next few years God gave me increased wealth and showed me His purpose for doing so.

To understand the transition from **Conquest** to **Power** you need to remember the following point: **You move into Power unknowingly when you continue to conquer new challenges**... the challenges of learning and of participating ... of being prepared and of helping to prepare others. **You slip out of Power when you stop conquering new challenges.**

When you are in Power you've got to pass your wealth on to others because God will not pour into hands that are already full.

God wants you to pass wealth on so that others can benefit from it. God works through people on earth to accomplish His purpose which sometimes is to pass along wealth. So how do you pass the wealth on? Where do you start?

Let's see how I started passing my wealth on.

As I drove into the parking lot, to the police officer directing traffic, we probably looked like any other father and son going to the Memphis Grizzlies basketball game ... just the two of us in my 2001 maroon Chevy Silverado 1500 truck. But for me it was a lot more than that. It was really an opportunity to empower my son Chip ... pass wealth along to him. He didn't know what I was doing ... only I did.

When Chip became a sophomore in high school I realized that I had only a small amount of time left to empower him before he went away to college and start receiving a large amount of his influence from individuals who I didn't know. I had always wanted him and his sister Dorian to learn from and be empowered by the experience that I had acquired years ago while I was **Stumbling Over A Quarter To Pick Up A Penny.** While thinking about how to pass that knowledge on to them I came up with the idea of ... Riding to the Games.

Experience told me that he would be best receptive if we were alone. The Memphis Grizzlies professional basketball team had just moved to town and Chip liked basketball so I bought season tickets and for 45 times each year during his sophomore, junior and senior years in high school we would be alone in my truck going to the Grizzlies games. In that truck, for me, it wasn't about *going* to the games ... it was about *being* there with him during this time in his life.

How did I use the trips to the game to empower Chip and pass along wealth to him? By taking those times to give him knowledge and allow him to digest it and question it. By taking the time to give him principles and then setting the stage for him to practice them and learn from his mistakes. By taking the time to give him the chance to observe how I interacted with the people that we came into contact with on those nights.

Chip learned and observed a lot during those trips to the game. He learned that I talked about the goodness of God just as easily on the way home from the games as I did on the way home from church on Sundays. He learned that I stood, placed my hand over my heart and removed my hat when The Star-Spangled Banner was played. He saw that I was courteous and said "please" and "thank you". He saw me open the door for ladies and the elderly.

He learned about time management because he had to have his homework done and his chores finished before we left. For me, I had to have my homework done too but it was a different kind of homework. My homework was to prepare the lesson that I would give to him that night on our trips to the game. Not a haphazardly prepared lesson ... but with purpose. Each lesson had to include some discussion of God. It had to strengthen his knowledge of his family ... beginning with his grandfather Joe L. Townsend Sr. and include information about his grandmother Bertha Mitchell Townsend who died when he was only two years old. The information had to provide some useful insight into the lives of his grandparents, uncles, aunts, cousins and other relatives ... where we came from and how we got here.

The lessons sometimes had to show him some of my faults and explain to him how I overcame them or at least how I stopped letting them control my life. He needed those lessons so that he would be prepared for life's failures and disappointments and have information to use to build solutions to his problems. I explained to him that God never disappoints but that his disappointments in life will come from man ... from other individuals or from himself.

The information about God and his family had to provide him bits of wisdom and direction that he could use to fill in some gaps for him when he matured. It had to prepare him for success by providing him with information that he could use to avoid periods of **Decline**, **Servitude** and **Probation** in his life, understand the **Conquest** and **Preparation** periods and finally enter into and prosper in sustained periods of **Power.** I taught him the **Six Spiritual Periods**.

In America and around the world the three years prior to the time of this story was the frighteningly mad Y2K technology push towards a year 2000 certain disaster. Because I had an Information Technology degree and over a decade of experience computer science job headhunters all over the globe were contacting me practically everyday with job offers. But accepting any one of them would have taken my wife Barbara and me away from Memphis and away from Chip and our daughter Dorian. Their biological mother and I were divorced but we shared joint custody and she wanted them to stay in Memphis. I was determined that they would have as normal of a childhood as possible so taking a job that would have required me to relocate to another city was out of the question. I had always wanted to live in Boston, London, Paris, Vancouver and other international cities so turning down positions in those places took a lot of self-control on my part.

I refused the career offers because throughout God's word it is clear that He intends for a father to be present in his children's lives to teach and train them. The father should provide for children the strength to match the sensitivity that the mother provides. A father should not only tell their children what they should do but he should be an example for them. So I asked myself this question: How could I be an example to Chip and Dorian if I was in Paris,

London, Atlanta or Philadelphia and they were in Memphis? As I mentioned earlier, I didn't have full custody of them so they would have had to remain in Memphis. I didn't take the offers because I didn't want Dorian to be one of the 50% of American teenage girls who become pregnant when their father is absent in their life. Nor did I want Chip to be in the 80% of teenage fatherless boys that fill our prisons. I just wanted to do the best that I could based on what God's word says that a father should do for his children ... I just wanted to be there and set the right example for them. I just wanted them to learn to live in God's **Power** and I had to be there to help them do it.

So every Grizzlies game during Chip's sophomore year we would get into my truck and drive to the basketball games and talk. Sometimes the conversation centered on him with me pulling information from him about the current events in his life or his goals or his dreams. Other times it centered on the lessons that I had prepared with me telling stories of my successes and failures or stories about his grandfather and grandmother, great-grandfathers and great grandmothers, uncles and aunts, cousins and his brother Jesus.

One night as we were leaving the house I said, "Chip I know that I've told you that your grandfather, Joe Sr., was a bricklayer who owned his own business, but did you know that he also was the organizer of many labor protests in the Mid-South during the fifties and sixties. So ... if you find yourself organizing a protest every now and then don't be too surprised. It's genetic." I told him how his uncle, Joe Jr., was one of the students who integrated Memphis State in the 1960s. I told him about how I became homeless when his grandfather died because I felt, incorrectly I might add, that I had no one that I could relate to. Then I gave him a little wisdom. I said, "Chip, if you ever feel like there's no one for you to relate to you just need to talk to your brother Jesus and together with Him pray to God."

Another conversation went like this, "Chip", I said, "what are you going to make your career?" He said, "Dad I haven't thought about that yet." We talked about careers in law, medicine business and other areas. And then I told him what Solomon said in Proverbs 16:3, "Commit to the LORD whatever you do and your plans will succeed." The conversation then moved to a discussion of his gifts. I told him, "Chip ... focus on what your gifts are and isolate one of them that you believe that you would enjoy using to provide your wealth ... then ... you need to commit it to the Lord and focus on developing it to its best potential." The following year he decided to pursue a career in business and made a commitment to work towards it. He started collecting *jars*, and his *jars* have been filling up with *oil* every since.

During Chip's senior year in high school I passed the baton to him so that he could take the lead position when we rode to the game. He had gotten his driver's license earlier that year so he drove and I rode. It was my turn to observe how he handled "grown-up" experiences ... and it didn't take long before I got a chance to see. It was on the first night that he drove his car, a 1993 white Dodge Shadow, to the game.

The sun was a gold semi-circle just about halfway below the horizon when Chip drove up the ramp to get on Bill Morris Parkway that heads west towards downtown. Thirty-five minutes later when we arrived downtown he went to the same parking lot that I had used when I drove us to the games. Since we always arrived early we could find decent free parking a couple of blocks from the stadium. Tonight was no different and we found our usual free parking spot.

The lot where we parked was in an area called the Pinch district. It is the original location of the first neighborhood in the city of Memphis. It was two blocks north of the Pyramid Arena on Front Street beside an old 1930's era warehouse that was under renovation. He parked his car and we got out and walked toward the arena. This area of the city is also where three of the Memphis' original town squares, Exchange, Market, and Auction continue to exist as grim reminders of the slavery trade that was used to help build the city that started back in 1819.

Our team took a beating that night. I don't remember who the visiting team was but during that time it could have been any one of the other 29 teams in the league. One thing that I had learned about Chip over the past two years was that he was loyal. No matter how bad we were getting beat he would never be one of the fans that hit the exit with five minutes left in the 4th quarter, even if we were down 25 points. He liked to stay until the end of the game. Maybe, just maybe, he was trying to spend as much time with me as possible. I'll have to ask him.

So when the final horn blew we left the Pyramid and walked the two blocks back to the car. When we got to the car I said, "Wow! ... look at that." Someone had broken out the rear opera window on the passenger side of the car. I then remembered that I had mistakenly left my cell phone in full view in the console tray. We got into the car, I mentioned that to him and then I turned to him and asked, "Well ... what did you learn from this?" He look at me and said, "Dad ... *you* should make sure that you take time to put your stuff away because people are out there to take it even when you think they are not." He looked at me and laughed and also said, "I shouldn't be too cheap to pay for good parking". The window cost $150.00 to replace. The secured parking in the lot across the street would have cost just $5.00. He had learned a lesson about not **Stumbling Over A Quarter To Pick Up A Penny**. The empowerment had begun in earnest.

During those rides I talked to him about God and His sovereign power. I told him, "Chip, everything seen and unseen belongs to God. Use the power that He has given you wisely, never isolate yourself from God or break your connection with Him." He smiled at me and said his usual, "Okay Pop."

One night when we talked I told him to continue to increase his knowledge never get lazy. Another night I talked to him about giving more than just his tithe to the church but give offerings too. I told him that the Bible says in Proverbs 11:25, "A generous man will prosper; he who refreshes others will himself be refreshed." I encouraged him to volunteer his time to help others. I said, "Chip, God doesn't pour more into hands that are full so you need to learn to give your time and money to help others." I know that doing these things will help him to stay in God's **Power**.

We also listened to the Hip Hop music that he normally played on the radio when he was alone or with his friends. He would move to change the station when he knew that the lyrics were going to be inappropriate but I told him not to change it so that we could discuss what the rappers were saying in their lyrics. When we discussed the songs I think that he learned a little wisdom about right and wrong and how to treat women.

I thank God for the time that He gave us together and I will always treasure it. When Chip reads this he will find out something that I didn't tell him during those three years of trips to the game. I'm sure that he doesn't know it because of what he did during the Christmas season of his freshman year in college in 2004 when he bought me a Grizzlies hat and tee shirt that he just knew that I would treasure. What he will find out when he reads this is that I wasn't a die-hard Grizzlies fan but I was and will always be a Chip fan and that we can ride to a Grizzlies' game in my old truck together anytime he wants too. *You see it wasn't about going to the game ... it was about being there.*

Let's talk about **Power**.

Here are two facts about getting into God's Power and remaining there: 1) In God's Power is where you want to spend your life and; 2) Getting to God's Power and staying in His Power is not as easy as it may seem. We'll take our time here.

Coming from a **Conquest** period you will be in God's **Power** before you realize that you're there and once you're there everything will seem to be working for you. When in the **Power** period you should be aware of God's sovereign **Power** and readily accept it. Remember what the Bible says in Proverbs 16:3, "Commit to the LORD whatever you do, and your plans will succeed."

It is your *obedience* to make the new conquests that God has for you that puts you in His Power. It is your *continued obedience* to make new conquests that keeps you in His Power.

Are You Ever Alone With God?

God continually tries to keep you in **Power** but sometimes you don't get the message for several reasons. Maybe it's because you have too much other *stuff in your car* with you when God wants to Ride to the Game with you *alone* and teach you lessons. That other *stuff in your car* keeps you from seeing how God has empowered you. That other stuff keeps you from seeing the wealth that He has caused you to have.

What does *alone* mean? *Alone* means without the radio on or you talking on your cell phone. *Alone* means just you and God without any crutches ... without the crutch of your positions and titles ... without the crutch of your family and friends ... without the crutch of counselors and confidants. All of those crutches keep you from learning how to lean on God alone. Are you your own crutch? Do you lean on your own understanding rather than following what the scripture says in Proverbs 3:5-9, " Trust in the LORD with all your heart and lean not on your own understanding; in all your ways acknowledge Him, and He will make your paths straight. Do not be wise in your own eyes; fear the LORD and shun evil. This will bring health to your body and nourishment to your bones."

The behavior that gets you into God's Power won't keep you in His Power.

The Children of Israel, experienced great wealth and power from the many conquests that God allowed them to achieve under the strong leadership of King David, his son Solomon and others. Those conquests put their nation in **Power** but those conquests alone could not keep them in God's **Power**. Here's a little bit about that time period.

After the death of Saul's son Ish-bosheth, David came to rule all of the tribes of Israel, creating a united Kingdom of Israel. When David died his son Solomon continued many of the good practices that David did including conquering new challenges and establishing meaningful political arrangements. Eventually Solomon's sin, including idolatry and turning away from God, led to his demise. When he died David's grandson Rehoboam succeeded him as king but he was rejected by ten of the twelve Tribes of Israel. This split the Kingdom just as God had promised Solomon he would do for building a high place for Chemosh the detestable god of the Moabites.

The split left the Southern Kingdom of Judah, made up of the tribes of Judah and Benjamin, to be ruled by the Davidic line. The Northern Kingdom of Israel, made up of the remaining ten tribes who followed a rebel named Jereboam, fell to the Assyrian Empire in 720 BCE because of, among other things, their disobedience and unrighteous living.

The Northern Kingdom fell because none of the 19 kings that ruled in the Northern Kingdom did what was right in the eyes of God. They stopped making wise choices and ignored any remnants of the wisdom that God had provided them with during the time that David and Solomon ruled. They didn't continue the customs or the conduct that kept them in **Power**.

The Book of Law that God had provided to them by Moses was lost. They stopped worshipping according to scripture. They willfully ignored and broke Judaic Laws and customs. They did not pay attention to any of these internal problems that were brought on after Solomon died. There was chaos and they did everything opposite of what they should have. They lost their **Power** and gradually went into **Decline** and wound up in **Servitude** with Satan setting their agenda.

On the other hand, the Southern Kingdom, the Kingdom of Judah, stayed in **Power** and survived intact for almost 150 years after the Northern Kingdom fell. It survived going into captivity until it was conquered in 586 BCE by the Babylonian Empire under Nebuzar-adan, captain of Nebuchadnezzar's body-guard.

Why did the Southern Kingdom survive intact longer than the Northern Kingdom did? It was because they continued to honor Judaic Law and be obedient to God. They continued the good conduct that enabled them to be blessed by God until they too finally had a series of kings that stopped conquering their surrounding enemy. The kings compromised their relationship with God by building improper relationships with their enemies. They turned their back on God and eventually stopped doing what was right in His eyes. That's where their **Power** ended and they too wound up in **Servitude** with Satan setting their agenda.

How's The Fruit?

To remain in God's Power you must know and use the power of the Fruit of the Spirit.

Conquest ushers you into the **Power** period. The behavior that keeps you in God's **Power** is found in what Apostle Paul writes is Gal 5: 22–27 that says, "But what happens when we live God's way? He brings gifts into our lives, much the same way that fruit appears in an orchard—gifts like affection for others, exuberance about life, serenity. We develop willingness to stick with challenges, a sense of compassion in the heart, and a conviction that a basic holiness permeates things and people. We find ourselves involved in loyal commitments, not needing to force our way in life, able to marshal and direct our energies wisely." In other words, we learn to grow up rather than just grow older ... we learn self-control.

How true were Paul's words. And during those trips to the game I tried to pass the wealth of the Fruit of the Spirit of love, joy, peace, longsuffering, kindness, goodness, faithfulness, gentleness and self-control to Chip. I told him that, "while God almost always gives a person more than one gift he should not try to develop more than one of them at a time and that if he did try to do that he would fail and none of them would be developed to their fullest potential."

Let's discuss self-control for a minute and how to use it to put the brakes on your slide from God's Power.

We should use self-control to keep us under the restrictions that allow us to flourish and remain in God's **Power**. We've got to get this right because we don't want to become carnal Christians. You know the ones that have the stinking attitude and worship idols rather than the real God. You know them ... they are the ones who won't step out in faith and are not only paranoid about everything but are impotent in almost all of their relationships. They lack self-control over their lives, their *fruit* is rotten and they will damage your *fruit* too. The old saying, "one bad apple spoils the whole barrel" is true.

Satan plays a big role in your sliding out of Power.

When you are in God's **Power** Satan attacks you at your strength. The attacks are not like the attack that takes place when you are attacked in **Decline**, **Servitude**, or **Probation**. They are calculated to be most effective and are usually internal in nature. Internal to your heart. Internal to your mind. Internal to your family and closest friends ... those that you love and those that you are certain that love you. You change immediately but you don't recognize that it is happening because you are still in God's **Power**. Satan uses many tools to attack you and one of his most effective ones is the death of a loved one.

Death Can Derail You

When a friend dies there are lots of questions that you think about asking them. When your father dies you don't want to talk to anyone.

Like most boys, my father Joe L. Townsend Sr. and I had a special relationship. He was a quiet man who taught me many life-long skills including discipline and organization. He was a World War II veteran and had become sick with several illnesses, including cancer and tuberculosis. From the time that I was ten years old he spent long periods of time in the hospital getting treatment and convalescing at home. Even after his health failed him he continued to be industrious. Although he couldn't do physical work any more, that didn't keep him from using his sharp mind to come up with lots of character-building projects for me and my sisters and brothers to do.

The last time that I saw him alive was at the Veteran's Administration hospital in Memphis when I kissed him on the forehead and said, "I love you dad ... I'll see you tomorrow." But tomorrow never came. The next time I saw him he was at the R. S. Lewis Funeral Home on Vance Street a few blocks south of Beale Street in downtown Memphis.

When I came to the hospital on what would have been the tomorrow ... I met my mother, brothers and sisters exiting through the south gate that led to the visitor's parking lot. Dad had died earlier that day while I had been in class at Memphis State. I felt so alone meeting them that way ... all by myself as I entered that parking lot gate ... me going one way and them going another. I felt that aloneness for quite some time. In the next few years I always seemed to be going in the opposite direction from them.

While they all got in their cars and headed to my mother's house, I got in my white 1974 Pontiac Lemans car, left the parking lot and drove west on Jefferson Street, South on Pauline Ave and east on Union Avenue to I-240. I took the south exit to get on the expressway and I drove south to the I-55 south exit. I took the I-55 exit south and I drove and drove and drove for the next 8 hours.

Unaware to me, a **Decline** period was about to begin in my life. My father's death had a tremendous impact on my life ... but what led to my fall from God's **Power** into **Decline** and later into **Servitude** wasn't my father's death ... it was the fact that I allowed his death to be used by Satan to internalize his attack on me. Looking back, I realize that I had already become *spiritually homeless* because I had stopped the behavior that God required of me to keep me in His **Power**. My behavior had become rotten and I had started discarding the Fruit of the Spirit like they were spoiled items that had gone bad since I picked them up at the market a few days ago. One by one after my father's death, I discarded love, joy, peace, longsuffering, kindness, goodness, faithfulness, gentleness and self-control. I isolated myself and discarded from my life those individuals that I could have depended on for support and I soon began experiencing the consequences of that choice.

If I had known about, or even better, understood the **Six Spiritual Periods** I would have given love, embraced joy, and been more peaceful and kind. I would have looked for ways to be good and show my faithfulness. I would have maintained my self-control. I would have known better than to isolate myself. If I had been able to produce the Fruit of the Spirit in me I would have been able lift myself out of my *spiritual homelessness* sooner ... or maybe I would have never experienced it at all because I don't believe that my homelessness at that time was God's Will.

To remain in God's Power you must honor God with your wealth by first giving to Him the first fruits of your crops and then by giving to others.

The Bible says in Proverbs 3:9-10, "Honor the LORD with your wealth, with the first fruits of all your crops; then your barns will be filled to overflowing, and your vats will brim over with new wine."

Here are a couple of more **Power** *actions.*

When you are in the God's Power whatever you do will be successful.

The Bible says in Psalms 1:1-3, "Blessed is the man who does not walk in the counsel of the wicked or stand in the way of sinners or sit in the seat of mockers. But his delight is in the law of the LORD, and on His law he meditates day and night. He is like a tree planted by streams of water, which yields its fruit in season and whose leaf does not wither. Whatever he does prospers." What God is saying here? He's saying that if you want to be successful "*don't hang around fools (recognized or unrecognized ones)*".

To remain in the God's Power you must strive to be *blameless* not perfect.

Are You Blameless?

The Bible says in Proverbs 28:6, "Better a poor man whose walk is *blameless* than a rich man whose ways are perverse." The Bible holds knowledge of many less than perfect men who God placed in His **Power**. *None* of them were perfect and neither will you be perfect ... but they were *blameless* and knew and understood the importance of praying to God for forgiveness. You must understand that you need to repent too and receive forgiveness when you have sinned against the Will of God.

One of the *blameless* men in the Bible was Noah who constantly walked with God. In our day, Noah's walk with God would probably be a ride in Noah's old truck where he and God would be alone and God would show him what His Will for him was. Here is what the Bible says in Genesis 6:8-10 about that *blameless* relationship. "But Noah found favor in the eyes of the LORD ... Noah was a righteous man, *blameless* among the people of his time, and he walked with God. Noah had three sons: Shem, Ham and Japheth." *Blameless* he was and God chose his seed through his sons, Shem, Ham and Japheth to re-people the earth. Now that's power.

Another *blameless* man was Job. The Bible says in Job 1:1, "In the land of Uz there lived a man whose name was Job. This man was *blameless* and upright; he feared God and shunned evil." Job continually prayed and worshipped God. He continually thanked Him for his blessings, which he considered to be everything good *and bad*

Understanding Your Life's Six Spiritual Periods

that came into his life. He would even offer prayers to God if he felt that his adult children had sinned against Him. God Himself called Job *blameless* in Job 2:3, "Then the LORD said to Satan, "Have you considered my servant Job? There is no one on earth like him; he is *blameless* and upright, a man who fears God and shuns evil. And he still maintains his integrity, though you incited me against him to ruin him without any reason."

And when God allowed Satan to test him, Job understood that he remained in God's Will. Even after his earthly possessions dwindled and his family was taken away he remained *blameless*. He had no way of knowing that God would restore him to **Power** and even increase his wealth to be more than it was before the tests .... but he remained *blameless*. You can learn a lot from Job.

So how do you become *blameless*? Let's look at another one of God's men in the Bible who sinned but knew what to do and see how he did it. Let's look at David a man who failed on numerous occasions, but was still a "man after God's own heart." In Samuel 22: 21-24 David writes, "The LORD has dealt with me according to my righteousness; according to the cleanness of my hands he has rewarded me. For I have kept the ways of the LORD; I have not done evil by turning from my God. All His laws are before me; I have not turned away from His decrees. I have been *blameless* before Him and have kept myself from sin." There are three key behaviors that you can learn from what David wrote:

1) Keep the ways of the LORD;

2) Don't do evil by turning away from God's decrees;

3) Do all that you can to keep yourself from sin.

To remain *blameless* and to stay in God's **Power** you need to do take the three actions listed above and when you make mistakes and sin ... you must repent and not allow your sin to lead you into **Decline** and **Servitude**.

Noah a drunkard but *blameless*. Job a tested wealthy man but *blameless*. David an adulterer and murderer but *blameless*. You see the pattern here ... they were not perfect but they were *blameless*. **You too must strive to be *blameless*.**

Stumbling Over A Quarter To Pick Up A Penny

Okay, now that we've discussed **Power** we've covered all **Six Spiritual Periods.** Let's move to the next chapter so that you can learn how to recognize them and use the power of their knowledge in your life.

Chapter Seven
Conclusion: How Do You Do It?

In the late 1980s and early 1990s I was well into my forties but I still was having a hard time ignoring the pennies of false prosperity and picking them up rather than identifying and holding on to the quarters that represented God's **Power**. One reason was because I was unwilling to give up the inappropriate behavior that had always given me pleasure and a temporary sense of power. I had picked up *crutches* that I didn't want to give up. Like my dependence on my education, the freedom I found in owning my own business, the creative expression that I enjoyed in playing music and the memory of the sheer excitement of the immoral experiences that I had been involved in years earlier.

Another reason why it took me so long to find my way was because I thought that I had figured life out. I had been a lot of places and seen and done a lot of things ... stumbled over a lot of quarters and picked up a lot of pennies. The truth was that I liked my stuff and I also liked my life just as it was. I enjoyed the scheming and false power that went along with me being my own boss and calling my own shots. I enjoyed the false sense of control that I had over my life. I liked coming and going when I chose to ... so I fiercely fought to maintain my independence even after I was sure that God had quarters for me in my future and all I had was pennies. My search for the pennies went on until one day God said, "Listen to me! I've had enough of your foolishness!"

Okay I'm listening ... I'm really, really, really listening this time.

God had said, "I've had enough of your foolishness" to me in the spring of 2003 the year of my 50th birthday. He didn't speak from heaven and shout His words at me. He used His Book, some events and several people that were in my life to blend together the message He had for me. Once the message was complete He tapped me on the shoulder when I was sitting under a Redwood tree outside of a vacation place in a resort that my wife and I were staying at in Napa Valley, California. I was enjoying myself reading the *Day of the Saints*, a book written by Dr. Bill Hamon. As I sat there reading, all of a sudden the relationship that God wanted me to have with Him became clear. All of the past guilt that I was holding on to that was hindering my relationship with Him and causing me to stumble and miss His Will for me went away. And for the first time in my adult life I seriously considered that God had something special for me to do and was not going to take no for an answer. It was also the first time as an adult that I acknowledged the words that my grandmother, Emma Mitchell, had told me 44 years earlier when she had said, "Boy ... you gonna be a preacher." Up until then I had not thought about what she had said since she had said it.

Dr. Hamon writes in his book that all Christians are ministers in the market place. Some are accomplished pulpitarians, some are teachers and others are placed in business to do God's Will there. I didn't see myself preaching in a pulpit but I could certainly entertain the idea of being a minister in the business marketplace or even a teacher.

So for the next few months I was confused and started backtracking. I foolishly debated the *preacher* idea until God said, "Hayward, the debate is over!" He said it to me on my birthday, Sunday, August 31st. I went to the altar to pray before worship service began and I asked God to give me a sign, right now, if He was truly *calling me* into the ministry. I told Him that I needed a *burning bush*. When I got up from the altar I took my seat and laid my Bible on my lap. When I opened it to begin reading there staring me in the face were the words in Isaiah 61:1-3 that read:

> "The Spirit of the Lord GOD is upon me; because the LORD hath anointed me to preach good tidings unto the meek; He hath sent me to bind up the brokenhearted, to proclaim liberty to the captives, and the opening of the prison to them that are bound; To proclaim the acceptable year of the LORD, and the day of vengeance

of our God; to comfort all that mourn; To appoint unto them that mourn in Zion, to give unto them beauty for ashes, the oil of joy for mourning, the garment of praise for the spirit of heaviness; that they might be called trees of righteousness, the planting of the LORD, that He might be glorified."

Seen Any Burning Bushes Lately?

The above verses were my *burning bush* and confirmed for me my call to ministry. I began to study God's word more intensely. A couple of years later I started teaching Church School classes on Saturday nights at my church and that's when God gave me the understanding of the **Six Spiritual Periods** that I have written about in this book.

After having spent time being both physically and spiritually homeless in the 1970s and early 1980s I looked at life differently during this period. I can remember that joy to me was having a bed to sleep in, some clean clothes and food to eat on a regular basis that came from a refrigerator that I owned or was at least buying on terms. I remember how I cherished the laughter of my young kids. But now my greatest joy is being able to recognize the important purpose that God has given to me ... and that is to share my knowledge of life's **Six Spiritual Periods.**

You can experience great joy too when you become able to quickly recognize which of the **Six Spiritual Periods** that you are presently in. The joy will come from your understanding of what you must do to live in God's **Power** or return to it if you are not there. You won't have to squander your wealth or your wisdom like I did by ***Stumbling Over A Quarter To Pick Up A Penny.*** You'll be in God's **Power** ... **and God's Power is that place where you experience victory after victory regardless of your circumstances**.

Here's how to do it.

Chapter Eight

Steps to Using the Understanding of the Six Spiritual Periods

Writing this book is one of the conquests that I am using to keep me in God's **Power.** Let's look at the steps that you should use to get to God's Power or remain there if you have already found your way there:

1) Determine The Spiritual Period That You Are In
2) Determine Your Restoration /Recovery Path
3) Determine What Action You Need To Take
4) Take The Action

Let's investigate them.

1) **Determine The Spiritual Period That You Are In**

Recognizing the correct period that you are in is the most critical step in understanding your life's **Six Spiritual Periods** and using that knowledge to work for you. Read the following list and use the information to determine the period that you are in based on what's happening in your life.

If you are in this:

Period	What Is God Doing To Or For You
Probation	God is challenging you to get rid of your self-defeating habits
Preparation	God is preparing you to meet life's conquests
Conquest	God is allowing you to expand and grow in to **Power**
Power	God is allowing you to achieve victory after victory
Decline	God is allowing your victories to end because you have stopped taking the actions necessary to keep you in His **Power**
Servitude	God is allowing difficulties and decay to enter your life because you are letting Satan set your agenda

2) Determine Your Restoration /Recovery Path

Remember the following facts: You can be in any one of life's **Six Spiritual Periods** at any given time but you can only be in one of them at a time. You don't have to go through the periods serially, one directly after the other, either. There is a Recovery Path that you should take based on the period you are in. What I'm saying is that if you are in **Servitude** you don't have to go through **Probation**, **Preparation** and **Conquest** to get to God's **Power**. Here are the Recovery Paths:

If you are in this: *Then you need to take this path:*

Period	Recovery Paths To God's Power
Probation	Take **Preparation** and **Conquest** to God's **Power**
Preparation	Take **Conquest** to God's **Power**
Conquest	Continue in **Conquest** until you arrive in God's **Power**
Power	Continue to conquer new challenges to stay in God's **Power**
Decline	Take **Preparation** and **Conquest** to get to God's **Power**
Servitude	Take **Probation, Preparation** and **Conquest** to get to God's **Power**

Understanding Your Life's Six Spiritual Periods

The following diagram illustrates the Recovery Paths to God's Power:

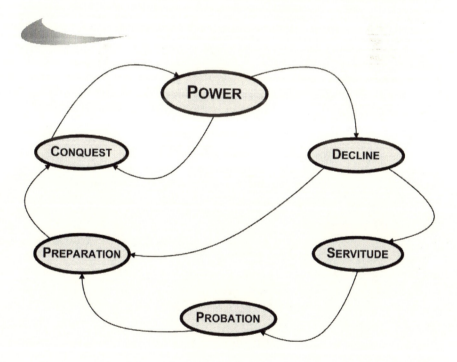

3) Determine What Action You Need To Take

The key to you getting to and remaining in what I will call the positive **Spiritual Periods** of **Preparation, Conquest** or **Power** depends on whether you are taking the right actions based on the period that you determined that you are in. If you are taking the wrong actions, not the ones determined from the **Determine The Spiritual Period That You Are In** section above, then you might as well be doing nothing.

If you have determined your current period correctly then you need to do the following:

1) Read the following list;
2) Use the information in it to tell you what actions to take.

If you are in this:

Period	The Action You Need To Take
Probation	You need to discard your old habits and embrace new ones
Preparation	You need to be learning new habits and hold on to what is good
Conquest	You need to fight to make rewarding experiences happen to you
Power	You need to continue to embrace the rewards of **Conquest**
Decline	You need to recognize that you are no longer in God's **Power**
Servitude	You need stop worshiping your idol gods (human and objects)

4) Take The Action

Because you might find yourself existing in any one of the **Six Spiritual Periods** at any given time making these simple concepts work for you may look like you are getting your life involved in a vicious circle. But that's not the case because the beauty of learning this process is that you don't have to go serially through the steps. All you need to do is use your knowledge of the **Six Spiritual Periods** to:

- Analyze your behavior and recognize what period you are in
- Identify the appropriate Recovery Path you need to take
- Determine what action you need to take based on the periods in your Recovery Path

- Take the action that you need to take

Using the knowledge of the **Six Spiritual Periods** may look likes it will take a lot of effort ... but since you're going to be putting forth the effort anyway you might as well be purposeful. Knowing what God wants you to be doing will make it easier.

God's People And The Six Spiritual Periods

Let's take a minute to identify some of the situations that God's people found themselves in in the Bible and see if we can relate them to the **Six Spiritual Periods** and see what God had them do.

God took his people in the Old Testament through the **Six Spiritual Periods.** It began with the Fall of Man when God moved Adam and Eve from the Garden of Eden and placed them on **Probation**. After centuries of Adam and Eve's oldest son Cain's descendants decline and decay He destroyed everyone on earth but Noah and his family in the Flood. He replenished the earth through Noah who was a descendant of Seth and who was Adam and Eve's replacement son for Abel who had been killed by his brother Cain.

To fulfill His promise to Abraham "to make him into a great nation", God moved Abraham's descendants, with Jacob and Joseph in charge into a **Preparation** period in Egypt to, among other reasons, save them from the Canaanites. There he allowed them to multiply from a nation of seventy to one that was, by some accounts, over 3 million in number. When He decided that they were prepared enough to leave 400 years later, He sent Moses to lead their exodus. After finishing their **Preparation** by allowing them to wander in the Desert for 40 years, God moved them into **Conquest** led by Joshua. They quickly defeated many enemies and moved into minimal **Power** while in a theocracy under the Judges and later total **Power** when David and Solomon reigned as kings.

They stayed in God's **Power** until they stopped worshipping God properly and doing the other things that had placed them in His **Power.** They began to allow the pagans who were around them to negatively influence their relationship with God and they began to move into **Decline**. They forgot the stories that Moses had recorded for them in Exodus 10:2 when the Lord said, "... tell your children and grandchildren how I dealt harshly with the Egyptians and how I performed my signs among them, and that you may know that I am the LORD." By forgetting those stories they forgot a major portion of their **Preparation** and fell into **Decline** and once in **Decline** they moved further away from God toward idol worship until they found themselves letting Satan set their agenda. Finally, they wound up in **Servitude** and God allowed the kingdom to split and them to fight against each other and later be taken captive by the Assyrians and Babylonians.

Mary's Story

Now I know that it is sometimes difficult to relate to stories that are thousands of years old like the one above ... so let's take a minute to read the story below about a young lady named Mary. Let's see if reading about Mary's experience can help you identify and understand the **Six Spiritual Periods**. As you read her story see if any part of it is familiar to you. If so highlight those parts in your book.

When Mary was first hired for her accounting position at the I Need a Better Job National Bank she had been struggling as a single mother of three to make ends meet. She had been underemployed, and working at Burger King for the past two years. She was in a **Probation** period in her life and while she had always prospered earlier, recently she had allowed relationships to lead her into **Decline**. While dealing in those relationships she had replaced a lot of good habits with bad ones and that had caused her to be in the situation she was in.

Mathematics, really any kind of work with numbers, was her gift and at the suggestion of a friend she began to attend a local junior college. Through her hard work she earned an associate's degree in accounting. While at the college she was in a positive environment and started to discard the bad habits that she had acquired in the past and replace them with good ones that she hadn't used in years. Once she began to use the good habits she began to feel better about her life and what the future could be for her children and her. Anyone who saw her accounting class work knew that she had finally found her gift. When she was offered the position at the I Need a Better Job National Bank she was prepared to succeed and conquer new challenges and it showed.

When Mary started her new job she would arrive at work on time and always displayed a very pleasant personality. When she had meetings to attend she arrived to them early, was always prepared to participate and made excellent contributions. She attended seminars that helped her to excel not only in her current position but they also positioned her for a promotion. She even volunteered for extra work.

Mary was unaware of it but God was moving her from **Probation** to **Preparation** on her job. He was allowing her to take the challenges found in that position to prepare her to move into **Conquest**. Her effort did not go unnoticed and after two years she got a promotion and continued to thrive. In **Conquest** she continued collecting *jars* to be filled with the wealth provided by God's *oil*. She went back to school to work on obtaining her bachelor's degree. She started to volunteer at several non-profit organizations around the community.

Mary then got a second promotion and when she got it got she entered into a **Power** period and that's when her problems started. She didn't handle the second promotion well. She had no knowledge of her life's **Six Spiritual Periods**. She didn't know that in order to continue to remain in God's **Power** she needed to continue to take the correct actions. She needed to take the ones that had helped to usher her into the **Power** period. She was getting ready to go *Stumbling Over A Quarter To Pick Up A Penny.*

What did Mary do wrong? She stopped fighting to make rewarding experiences happen to her in her life. How did that happen? She met a man and began a relationship with him. He became her *god* and the filter between her and God's **Power.** He told her that additional education was a waste of time and money ... so she stopped going to school. He told her that volunteering was a waste of time ... so she resigned from the boards that she had volunteered to participate on. Whenever she was away doing something to expand her gifts he told her that it was keeping them from spending time together even though he was never there when she was home. She became isolated and moved into **Decline**.

Once Mary fell into **Decline** she was attracted to the negative people at work and got with a group of them who attacked her at her strength. They gossiped and criticized the people she had to work with on a daily basis and that left her in the awkward position of having to be a person that dealt in phony relationships. You know the kind that smile in your face and talk about other people when you are around and then smile in their face and talk about you when you are not around. That wasn't the kind of person that she really was, so to keep from feeling awkward about having to work in that situation she stop going to the meetings where the people who were gossiped about were. What she did was to replace the "motivated going somewhere" associates with the "can't do nothing, don't want you or themselves to have nothing" friends. She thought that she had made her life easier by not facing up to the gossips but what she had done was stop performing the fruitful habits that needed to be done to keep her in **Power**.

Mary was not a weak adolescent child but a strong-willed adult and she should have not fallen into that trap. What was her problem then? Her problem was the she didn't fully understand that Satan attacks strong individuals at their strengths. She never asked herself the question, "Why should Satan waste time irritating me at my weak points when he can devastate me all at once by attacking me at my strengths?" Satan had begun to wreak havoc in her life again like he had done a few years earlier and she had no idea that she was under attack.

Mary was having what I called in chapter three the "Psychic Plowboys Experience". She was dealing with duplicity. God was still blessing her and she was making bad decisions. She was doing things for the wrong reason and staying in her current situation longer than she should have stayed. She had stopped her conquest of the challenges that she had been successfully facing. She was staying in the relationship with that parasite of a man that she had picked up way too long and he was isolating her.

God was willing to put Mary on **Probation** and wait for her to work her way out of the situation and back to the place where He intended for her to be ... but because she didn't know what actions to take to stop the slide, Mary became depressed and she felt trapped. And even though just a few months earlier she had felt that her life was on track for bigger achievements ... she could do nothing that gave her life joy or head off the coming depression. When she tried to manage what was now happening in her life by the old ways that she was used to using she just made matters worse. Rather than giving control to God and letting Him place her on **Probation**, like an understanding of life's **Six Spiritual Periods** dictates, she tried to control what was happening to herself and that behavior allowed Satan, who worked through her boyfriend and coworkers, to set her agenda and she fell into **Servitude.**

Mary asked herself, "What's the point?" Just like any person who continuously diets and their clothes still don't fit any better, she told herself, "It won't do any good for me to try to accomplish anything. I had my chance. I'm stuck in this dead end place in my life. I might as well take the mess that my man, my friends and my family dish out." So unknowing she fell back to worshipping her job, her car, her fur coat, her children and all of the other idols that she had enjoyed but not worshipped during her **Conquest** period.

From that point on she yielded to her past weakness in the same way that the dieter yields to the bowl of ice cream or the bag of potato chips once they don't see any immediate results from their dieting effort. She became disgusted at herself for losing control of her life. She is unaware that when she was in **Power** Satan had attacked her at her strength and he was now setting her agenda. And because she wasn't using the power found in the understanding and use of the **Six Spiritual Periods** her effort to turn her life around was like trying to put out an electrical fire with water ... " it just doesn't work and only makes it worse". Totally spiritually defeated she now sits idle and unapproachable because she doesn't know how to move forward. She turns her back on God and is *Stumbling Over A Quarter To Pick Up A Penny.*

How Mary Returned To God's Power

Does Mary's story sound familiar? Of course it does and you know many people that are in situations just like her.

But there was hope for Mary. One day a friend gave her a copy of the **Six Spiritual Periods.** She read it and studied the concepts and saw in them a possible solution for her situation. She filled out the **Determining Your Life's Spiritual Period Worksheet** in the back and here's what happened.

First Mary analyzed her situation to determine what **Spiritual Period** she was in. Knowing that information would tell her what her **Restoration / Recovery Path** should be. Since she had a defeatist attitude and was letting Satan set her agenda; she knew that she was in **Servitude**. She wanted to be in **Power** so the first action that she took was to ...

Stop letting Satan set her agenda by discarding the negativity in her life.

Once she stopped letting Satan set her agenda she looked at the next step in the **Restoration / Recovery Path**. It said that for her to get out of **Servitude** she needed to get herself to **Conquest** and that she could accomplish that by going through the cleansing of the **Probation** period and the learning found in the **Preparation** period. She would first need to go through **Probation** and would start her recovery by ...

Discarding her old bad habits and embracing good new ones.

In **Probation** Mary submitted herself to God's Sovereign Will and began discarding her old habits and embracing new ones. When she changed her habits the influence of her old gossiping friends and controlling boyfriend was removed from her life. They left because of what it says in the Bible in James 4:7, "Submit yourselves, then, to God. Resist the devil, and he will flee from you." With that negative influence gone Mary moved from **Probation** to **Preparation**.

A short time later, while in **Preparation**, Mary started focusing on the gifts that God had placed in her life. She felt confident that she could again start having positive victories and rewarding experiences. That awareness and attitude told her that she was in the beginning of a **Conquest** period and that all that she needed to do was ...

Start fighting to make rewarding experiences happen in her life.

So Mary began to fight and through her effort she began to receive victories and rewards from those victories. Because she now understood her life's **Six Spiritual Periods**[3], she knew that she was in God's **Power.** She now believed that everything that she would do would be successful according to His Will for her. But while she was extremely happy, she had anxiety and was fearful of slipping out of God's **Power** again ... so she went back and read again what she needed to do to stay in God's **Power** and made a promise to herself to follow what it said. It said," If you are in God's **Power** you can stay there if you grow your Fruit of the Spirit by identifying and taking action on God's next challenges for you." Having read that she knew that she needed to:

Continue to conquer new challenges while living in and enjoying the Fruit of the Spirit.

Like Mary you can easily make a move to recover from your life's trials. While the complete recovery won't happen overnight, the process is just as simple as it is in her story and if you are willing to just understand and use the knowledge of the **Six Spiritual Periods** you can see dramatic changes almost immediately in your life.

J. Matthew Barrie, the Scottish author and dramatist who is best remembered for Peter Pan, the boy who refused to grow up, once wrote, "The life of every man is a diary in which he means to write one story, and writes another; and his humblest hour is when he compares the volume as it is with what he hoped to make it."[4] Don't let your life be reflected in his quote by *Stumbling Over A Quarter To Pick Up A Penny.*

Determining Your Life's Spiritual Period Worksheet

The LORD bless you and keep you; the LORD make his face shine upon you and be gracious to you; the LORD turn his face toward you and give you peace. (Numbers 6:24-26)

Determining Your Life's Spiritual Period Worksheet ©

Since you may be in any one of the **Six Spiritual Periods** you can list them in any order:

1) _____
2) _____
3) _____
4) _____
5) _____
6) _____

1) Determine The Spiritual Period That You Are In
Analyze yourself and list the **Spiritual Period** that you are currently in:
_____
_____

2) Determine Your Restoration /Recovery Path
List your Restoration / Recovery Path based on the **Spiritual Period** that you are currently in:
_____
_____

3) Determine What Action You Need To Take
Referring to your Restoration / Recovery Path written above list the action(s) that you should take to get back to God's **Power**:
_____
_____
_____

4) Take The Action
Take the actions that you listed above in step 3 and move back to God's **Power**.

Hayward C. Townsend Sr.   haywardtownsend.com

May God continue to bless you mightily ....

Hayward C. Townsend Sr.
CEO, Faith Enterprises, LLC
Websites: haywardtownsend.com; yourfaithenterprises.com
Contact: haywardht@aol.com; 901.830.1711

Pictures

Then the LORD said to Moses, "Go to Pharaoh, for I have hardened his heart and the hearts of his officials so that I may perform these miraculous signs of mine among them that you may tell your children and grandchildren how I dealt harshly with the Egyptians and how I performed my signs among them, and that you may know that I am the LORD." (Exodus 10:1-2)

"Dad"
My father Joe L. Townsend Sr.
in his military uniform in the early 1940s.

"Mom"
My mother Bertha M. Townsend about the age she was
when she swept my dad off his feet.

"Granny"
My grandmother Emma Mitchell in her 90s.
She lived to be 103 years old.

"Barb"
My wife Barbara at about the time when
she swept me off of my feet.

"Dori T"
Our daughter Dorian at time of her high school graduation in 2006.

"Chip"
Our son at the time of his high school graduation in 2004.

"The Baby Eagles"
My sisters Carol, Mamie and Marion seated in front of me, Rick and Joe, my brothers, in the mid-1970s when I was in **Decline**.

"Ordination"
My ordination service in 2004. Dr. Adkins who is officiating,
my sister Overseer Marion Douglas, Pastor Douglas Brook,
Pastor Gino Dennis and me ...
when I had made my way back to God's **Power**.

"The Psychic Plowboys"
Starring: "Lonesome" Dave Blair, The Reverend Doctor Daniel Morris Hopper, Eric Phillips and Hayward Carfield Townsend in the spring of 1994 when I was on **Probation**.

Endnotes

Chapter Three
Probation: The Psychic Plowboys Experience

1. Og Mandino, *The Greatest Secret In The World* (New York.: Bantam Books, 1972), p. 11.

Chapter Four
Preparation: Baby Eagles and Piano Lessons

2. Chuck R. Swindoll, *Moses: A Man of Selfless Dedication* (Nashville: Thomas Nelson Publishers, 1999), p. 37.

Chapter Seven
Conclusion: How Do You Do It?

3. Orrin Root, Training for Service (Cincinnati.: Standard Publishing, 1996), p.41.
4. James M. Barrie, *The Little Minister*, 1891.

Acknowledgements

I take this time to acknowledge my sisters Mamie, Marion and Carol and brothers Joe and Rick and also all of my brothers-in-law, sisters-in-law, other family members and friends for richly adding to my life.

I'd like to thank my friends at AuthorHouse for your assistance in publishing ... you guys are simply outstanding.

Lucy ... thank you for your design and technical help ... you do such an excellent job providing creative work.

Dorian and Chip ... thank you for your editing and proofing help. Both of you are so brilliant and I love you dearly.

And I'm truly grateful to Barbara, my wife, the love of my life.

Faith Enterprises, LLC

-- Building People and Prosperity --

Seminars and Workshops

THE SIX SPIRITUAL PERIODS - a seminar that teaches you how to remain in God's **Power** while dealing with life's everyday challenges.

THE DRIVING LESSON - a seminar designed to teach you the principles and truth that every Mother and Father MUST tell their Daughter.

Preparing Your Child For Success - a workshop designed specifically to empower middle class parents with simple ways to prepare their children to excel for a lifetime.

On the Sixth Day: Leadership Seminar - a series of workshops designed to develop church leaders.

Using Leverage to Put Your Life in Motion - a workshop that shows you how to get the most out of God's blessings throughout your life.

Professional Services

Real Estate Sales and Development
Financial Planning
Retirement Planning
Tax consulting
Business Development

Books and Publications

Preparing Your Child For Success Workbook

Call or email us for more information about seminar details and booking information:

haywardht@aol.com
901.830.1711

Go to the following sites for more information:

yourfaithenterprises.com
haywardtownsend.com

Preparing Your Child For Success

"The most important workbook that Parents and Grandparents will complete for their child or grandchild."

- ✓ Learn the simple steps required to prepare your child to excel for a lifetime.
    - ✓ Why is this information important to you? It can mean $100,000+ to you and your family.
- ✓ For Parents & Grandparents of children (3 years and up).

Author: Hayward C. Townsend Sr.
Executive Pastor,
Greater Imani Church and Christian Center
CEO, Faith Enterprises, LLC
(For more information go to yourfaithenterprises.com, hywardtownsend.com. or contact us at haywardht@aol.com or 901.830.1711)

"Train a child in the way he should go, and when he is old he will not turn from it."

About The Author

Hayward C. Townsend Sr. is the Executive Pastor at Greater Imani Church and Christian Center in Memphis, Tennessee and CEO of Faith Enterprises, LLC.

Over the years, Pastor Townsend's work for God has taken him around the world to numerous countries in Western Europe, Africa, and the Caribbean. His careers in Engineering, Information Technology, Construction, Real Estate development and music have taken him to every corner of this country.

Pastor Townsend has over 30 years experience in local, national and international community and civic involvement. He is a past member of the board of directors for the International Association of Quality Circles (IAQC), Alliance for the Mentally Ill (AMI), Dover Elevator Credit Union and Memphis Youth Performing Arts Company (MYPAC).

He currently serves on the Program Advisory Committee for Remington College – Memphis Campus. Other current and former affiliations include the Project Management Institute (PMI), Black Professional Data Processing Association (BDPA) and the American Society of Certified Engineering Professionals (ASCET).

Through his business, **Faith Enterprises, LLC**, he and his wife offer personal, family, business and church-related seminars and workshops. Some of which include: **On the *Sixth Day: Leadership Seminar*** - a series of workshops designed to develop church leaders and ***Preparing Your Child for Success*** - a workshop designed specifically to empower middle class parents with simple ways to prepare their children to excel for a lifetime. ***Using Leverage to Put Your Life in Motion*** - a workshop that shows you how to get the most out of God's blessings throughout your life.

Pastor Townsend lives in Arlington, Tennessee, a suburb of Memphis, with his wife Barbara and their two college age children Dorian and Chip (Hayward II).

We Would Like To Hear From You

If you have a testimony to share
after reading this book please:

email me: hawardht@aol.com
twitter me: twitter.com/haywardtownsend
contact me on facebook: facebook.com/hayward.townsend

Additional copies of this book including
e-book format are available at:

haywardtownsend.com
yourfaithenterprises.com
major booksellers including Amazon.com, BarnesandNoble.com and the AuthorHouse online book store.

COMING SOON!!!

THE DRIVING LESSON
*What Every Mother and Father
MUST Tell Their Daughter*

"*Principles and truth to use for a lifetime.*"

Go to haywardtownsend.com for more information.

Lord Thank You Everyday©

Lord thank You for watching over me,
Lord thank You for setting my spirit free,
Lord thank You ... You mean so much to me,
Lord thank You.
Lord thank You.

Lord thank You each and every day,
Lord thank You for showing me the way,
Lord thank You ... You mean so much to me,
Lord thank You.
Lord thank You.

Lord Thank You Everyday.

Hayward C. Townsend Sr.
– June 2009-